PUB GRUB

recipes for classic comfort food

PUB GRUB

recipes for classic comfort food

RYLAND PETERS & SMALL
LONDON • NEW YORK

Art Director Leslie Harrington
Designer Geoff Borin
Editorial Director Julia Charles
Editor Alice Sambrook
Head of Production Patricia Harrington
Publisher Cindy Richards

Indexer Vanessa Bird

Published in 2021 by Ryland Peters & Small
20–21 Jockey's Fields   341 E 116th St
London WC1R 4BW   New York NY 10029

www.rylandpeters.com

Recipe collection compiled by Julia Charles.
Text © Miranda Ballard, Fiona Beckett, Jordan
Bourke, Tori Finch, Mat Follas, Emmanuel
Hadjiandreau, Tori Haschka, Carol Hilker,
Vicky Jones, Kathy Kordalis, Jenny Linford,
Hannah Miles, Laura Santini, Jenny Tschiesche,
Laura Washburn 2021.

Design and photographs © Ryland Peters & Small
2021. See page 144 for full text and image credits.

ISBN: 978-1-78879-381-0

10 9 8 7 6 5 4 3 2 1

Printed and bound in China.

CIP data from the Library of Congress has been
applied for. A CIP record for this book is available
from the British Library.

MIX
Paper from
responsible sources
FSC® C106563
FSC
www.fsc.org

41

Notes

• Both British (metric) and American (imperial
plus US cups) measurements are included in these
recipes; however, it is important to work with one
set of measurements and not alternate between
the two within a recipe.

• All eggs are medium (UK) or large (US), unless
specified as large, in which case US extra-large
should be used. Uncooked or partially cooked eggs
should not be served to the very old, frail, young
children, pregnant women or those with
compromised immune systems.

• Ovens should be preheated to the specified
temperatures. We recommend using an oven
thermometer. If using a fan-assisted oven, adjust
temperatures according to the manufacturer's
instructions.

CONTENTS

LIGHT BITES 8

MEATY MAINS 34

FISH DISHES 66

VEGGIE OPTIONS 86

SIDES AND SAUCES 106

DESSERTS 126

Index 142

Credits 144

INTRODUCTION

What can be better than recreating the ultimate comfort food in the sanctuary of your own home? Whether you are cooking for a few, preparing a candlelit dinner for two or just looking to practice a bit of culinary self-care, you'll find something to tempt you away from the takeaway menu and into the kitchen here.

So, what are the hallmarks of pub grub? It's traditional fare – sometimes with a modern flare – but always based around crowd-pleasing dishes that have stood the test of time for a reason. Read this cookbook like a menu full of hugs in edible form, and go for what makes you happy in the moment – whether that's pie, chips and curry sauce, burgers or oysters. This is the type of food that speaks to your soul, so embrace that comfort!

Pub grub doesn't have to be consumed with a drink, of course, but it just so happens that many of these meals go well with an alcoholic beverage. From lamb shanks with red wine, to burgers and beer, to mussels with white wine. Because the best of us know that eating isn't cheating, it actually turns a good evening with a bottle of wine into a great one.

Flick through the Soups and Light Bites section to find a tasty morsel such as Scotch Quails' Eggs to whet your appetite (see page 24). Peruse the Meaty Mains for substantial dishes such as Smoky Red Wine Short Ribs (see page 41). Sample one of the tempting Fish Dishes like Posh Fish Finger Sandwiches (see page 76). There are meat-free meals galore in the Veggie Options chapter, such as Mushroom Mac and Cheese (see page 88). Sides and Sauces are an integral part of the equation, try Triple-cooked Chips (see page 108). Finally, pick a perfect Dessert such as the Brownie Cheesecake (see page 139) to finish your meal in style. All this pub grub will be down the hatch before you can think twice.

chapter 1

LIGHT BITES

2 tablespoons sunflower oil

½ onion, chopped

1 leek, finely chopped

1 sprig of fresh thyme, leaves only

500 g/1 lb. field mushrooms, stalks trimmed and chopped

1 potato, peeled and diced

a splash of Madeira or Amontillado sherry

700 ml/3 cups chicken stock/broth

salt and freshly ground black pepper

freshly ground nutmeg

1 tablespoon olive oil

200 g/6½ oz. chestnut/cremini mushrooms, sliced, to serve

double/heavy cream, to garnish

finely chopped fresh chives, to garnish

garlic croutons

2 tablespoons olive oil

1 garlic clove, peeled

2 slices of day-old rustic bread, crusts trimmed off, cut into small cubes

serves 4

There is something very comforting about a good mushroom soup, with its particular earthy flavour and smooth richness. Here, garlicky croutons and freshly-fried chestnut/cremini mushrooms are a simple but effective way of adding a flavour and texture boost to this classic soup

mushroom soup

Heat the sunflower oil in a large saucepan over a medium heat. Add the onion, leek and thyme leaves and fry gently, stirring now and then, for 5 minutes until softened. Add the field mushrooms and fry, stirring, for 3 minutes until lightly browned.

Mix in the diced potato, then add the Madeira or sherry and cook, stirring, for a minute. Pour in the chicken stock/broth and bring to the boil. Reduce the heat, cover and simmer for 25 minutes.

Meanwhile, make the croutons. Heat the olive oil in a frying pan/skillet over a medium heat. Add the garlic clove and fry briefly until fragrant. Add the cubes of bread and fry until golden brown and crisp, discarding the garlic clove when it browns.

Blend the soup until smooth in a food processor or using a hand-held stick blender. Season with salt, freshly ground pepper and nutmeg. Bring to a simmer again in the saucepan to heat through.

When ready to serve, heat 1 tablespoon of olive oil in a frying pan/skillet over a medium-high heat. Fry the chestnut/cremini mushrooms until lightly browned.

Serve the warm soup in bowls, garnished with a swirl of double/heavy cream, some hot fried mushrooms, garlic croutons and chopped chives.

2 tablespoons extra-virgin olive oil

4 garlic cloves, crushed

1 onion, chopped

1 cauliflower, cut into florets

1 potato, peeled and chopped

500 ml/2 cups vegetable stock/broth

250 ml/1 cup unsweetened plant-based milk

4 tablespoons nutritional yeast (or to taste)

salt and freshly ground black pepper

to serve

1 tablespoon unsweetened oat cream or dairy-free cream

handful of finely chopped fresh chives

handful of pea shoots

crushed green peppercorns

serves 4

Why should our plant-based pals have to miss out on pub grub? This recipe is vegan heaven in a bowl! It contains nutritional yeast, which gives a deliciously savoury, cheesy flavour without the use of dairy.

cream of cauliflower soup

Heat the oil in a large saucepan and add the garlic and onion.

Cook over a medium-high heat until golden brown. Add the cauliflower, potato, stock/broth and milk and bring to the boil. Cook over a medium-high heat for about 15–20 minutes, or until the cauliflower is soft.

Add the nutritional yeast and some salt and pepper. Blend the soup until smooth in a food processor or using a hand-held stick blender. Serve with a swirl of oat cream and a sprinkling of chopped chives, fresh pea shoots and crushed green peppercorns.

2 bacon rashers/slices,
cut into thin strips

50 g/3½ tablespoons butter

1 onion, chopped

1 celery stalk, thinly sliced

1 heaped tablespoon flour

500 ml/2 cups full-fat/
whole milk

500 ml/2 cups
fish stock/broth

400 g/14 oz. floury potatoes,
peeled and diced

grated fresh nutmeg

500 g/1 lb. cod or other white
fish fillets, skinned and cut into
2.5-cm/1-inch cubes

200 g/1½ cups frozen
sweetcorn kernels

200 g/6 oz. cooked peeled
prawns/shrimp

2 tablespoons
chopped fresh parsley

salt and freshly ground
black pepper

serves 4–6

A tasty version of a classic New England soup. The soft potato and the delicate-textured cod and prawns/shrimp make it at once gentle and satisfying. Serve it for a hearty lunch or light dinner.

cod, sweetcorn and prawn chowder

In a large, heavy-based saucepan, fry the bacon, stirring, for 2 minutes. Add the butter and once it foams, add the onion and celery. Fry gently for 2–3 minutes until soft. Mix in the flour, stirring in well, and fry briefly.

Gradually stir in the milk first, then the fish stock/broth. Bring to the boil while stirring and cook until thickened.

Add the diced potatoes and simmer for 5–10 minutes until they are tender. Season with nutmeg, salt and freshly ground black pepper.

Bring to the boil, add the cod or other white fish and sweetcorn and simmer for 3–5 minutes until the fish is cooked. Add the prawns/shrimp and simmer for 2 minutes. Serve topped with parsley and extra freshly ground black pepper.

30 g/2 tablespoons butter

1 onion, chopped

1 celery stalk, chopped

1 large carrot,
peeled and chopped

400 g/2 cups dried green or
yellow split peas, soaked
overnight and then drained

1 small ham hock
(approximately 500 g/1 lb.)

salt and freshly ground
black pepper

serves 4

This delightful soup is what you need to eat by the fire after a long walk out in the cold. If the ham hock is very salty, soak it in water overnight before using, and discard the water.

split pea and ham soup

Melt the butter in a large saucepan and fry the onion, celery and carrot over a medium-low heat until soft.

Add the drained split peas to the pan, together with the ham hock and 1.8 litres/7 cups of water. Cover and bring to the boil, then reduce the heat and simmer for about 2 hours, or until the meat is falling off the bone and the peas are breaking down into the liquid.

Remove the ham hock from the pan with two forks and carefully strip off the skin, gristle and fat. Lift the meat off the bone and cut it into bite-sized chunks.

If you like a smooth soup, blend it in a food processor or using a hand-held stick blender, then return it to the pan, add the ham and reheat. If you like a chunky soup, then just return the ham hock chunks to the pan. You might like to reserve a little ham for topping the bowls of soup. Season to taste with salt and freshly ground black pepper and serve.

fries

Triple-cooked Fries
(see page 108)

curry sauce

2 tablespoons vegetable oil, plus
extra if needed

1 onion, grated

1 apple, peeled and grated

1 garlic clove, crushed

2-cm/¾-inch piece of fresh
ginger, peeled and grated

2 tablespoons medium-hot
curry powder

1 teaspoon ground turmeric

1 teaspoon paprika

2 teaspoons ground cumin

½ teaspoon ground coriander

1 tablespoon plain/
all-purpose flour

500 ml/2 cups chicken or
vegetable stock/broth

1 teaspoon Worcestershire
sauce

1 tablespoon tomato
purée/paste

freshly squeezed lemon juice
and/or sugar, to taste

serves 4

This is a British staple that's hugely popular comfort food for a reason – it's delicious! Depending on how hot you like your curry, adjust the curry-powder heat in the recipe and a good pinch of chilli/hot red pepper flakes as well if desired. Great with an ice-cold lager as a Saturday night treat.

curry fries

Prepare the curry sauce. Heat the oil in a large non-stick frying pan/skillet with the onion. Cook over a medium heat, stirring occasionally, until aromatic, 3–5 minutes. Add the apple, garlic, ginger, curry powder, turmeric, paprika, cumin and coriander and cook, stirring, for about 1 minute.

Add the flour, add a splash more oil if it is very dry, and cook, stirring continuously for another minute.

While stirring, gradually pour in the stock/broth and stir until well blended. Bring just to the boil, then reduce the heat to a simmer. Stir in the Worcestershire sauce and tomato purée/paste and simmer for 15 minutes. Taste. Depending on preference, add some lemon juice for more acidity or a pinch of sugar to sweeten, or both.

Blend the curry sauce until smooth in a food processor or using a hand-held stick blender. Set aside while you prepare the fries (see page 108).

To serve, reheat the curry sauce. Pile the fries onto plates and pour over the sauce. Serve immediately.

beer-battered cauliflower

750 ml–1 litre/3–4 cups vegetable oil

225 g/1¾ cups self-raising/rising flour

360 ml/1½ cups lager

1 cauliflower, cut into florets

plain/all-purpose flour, seasoned, for dusting

shoestring courgette/zucchini fries

3 large courgettes/zucchini

about 400 ml/1¾ cups full-fat/whole milk

about 400 g/3 cups plain/all-purpose flour, seasoned

salt and freshly ground black pepper

lemon wedges, to serve

serves 4

Look no further for the perfect alternative to fish and chips on a Friday. Beer batter makes everything better, including cauliflower.

beer-battered cauliflower with shoestring courgette fries

Preheat the oil in a deep fat fryer or large heavy-based saucepan to 180°C (350°F). When a cube of bread dropped in sizzles, browns and rises to the surface, then it should be ready.

For the beer batter, place the self-raising/rising flour in a bowl and whisk in the lager until a smooth batter forms. Dust the cauliflower with seasoned flour, dusting off any excess, then dip in the batter, shaking off any excess.

Deep-fry in batches, turning occasionally with a slotted spoon, until crisp and cooked through, about 3–4 minutes. Drain on kitchen paper and keep warm until ready to serve.

For the shoestring courgette/zucchini fries, finely julienne the courgettes/zucchini to make strings.

Carefully dredge the courgette/zucchini strings in the milk, then drain and shake around in the seasoned flour to lightly coat.

Lower the courgette/zucchini fries into the hot oil in batches and cook for 3 minutes or until light golden brown. Remove using a slotted spoon and drain the oil on kitchen paper.

Serve the beer-battered cauliflower and courgette/zucchini fries with plenty of salt and pepper and lemon wedges.

1 large baking potato

1 tablespoon olive oil

80 g/3 oz. pancetta cubes

1 tablespoon butter

40 g/scant ½ cup Cheddar cheese, grated

1 spring onion/scallion, trimmed and finely chopped

salt and freshly ground black pepper

serves 1

These loaded potatoes are a perfect party food but are equally good as an individual portion. You can flavour the filling with anything you choose really. This recipe calls for bacon, spring onion/scallion and Cheddar cheese, but you could use blue cheese and red onion or chorizo chunks and Manchego. Basically, anything super cheesy is a winner!

loaded jacket skins

Preheat the oven to 200°C (400°F) Gas 6.

Prick the skin of your potato and rub with olive oil. Place in the preheated oven for about 1 hour, depending on the size of your potato. To test if the potato is cooked, insert a sharp knife and if the potato feels soft inside with no resistance to the knife, it is done. If you still feel some resistance, cook for a little while longer.

Towards the end of cooking time, place the pancetta in a dry frying pan/skillet and fry, stirring regularly, for about 5 minutes until crisp and slightly golden. You do not need to add any oil when cooking as the pancetta will render fat as it cooks. Leave to cool slightly.

When the potato is cool enough to handle, carefully cut into quarters and scoop away most of the soft potato flesh, leaving the skins with enough potato on so that they hold their quarter shape. Place the scooped-out potato flesh in a bowl with the butter, season with salt and pepper and mash well. Add the pancetta pieces, most of the cheese, reserving a little to sprinkle on top, and the spring onion/ scallion and stir everything together.

Preheat the grill/broiler to high.

Place spoonfuls of the potato mixture back into each potato skin and place on a baking sheet. Sprinkle with the reserved cheese and place under the preheated grill/broiler for about 5 minutes until the cheese starts to turn golden brown. Serve straight away.

12 quails' eggs

600 g/20 oz. good quality pork sausages

1 tablespoon finely chopped fresh parsley

1 tablespoon finely chopped fresh thyme, leaves only (optional)

1 egg yolk, beaten, plus 1 whole egg

1 tablespoon plain/all-purpose flour

4 tablespoons full-fat/whole milk

75 g/1 cup fine breadcrumbs

sunflower oil, for frying

salt and freshly ground black pepper

makes 12

Bite-sized Scotch eggs are so much easier to eat with a drink than the bigger variety. A nice way to serve them is to mix a little mustard with mayo and serve on the side as a dip.

Scotch quails' eggs

Bring a small saucepan of water to the boil and gently lower in the quails' eggs. Boil for 1 minute 40 seconds, then plunge the boiled eggs immediately into cold water to stop the cooking process.

Once cold, one at a time, roll each egg gently along a work surface with the flat of your palm until the shell is all crackled, then peel away the shell. Set the peeled eggs aside until needed.

Remove the skins from the sausages and discard and put the sausage meat in a large mixing bowl with the parsley, thyme, if using, and egg yolk. Season with salt and pepper and stir to combine. Divide the mixture into 12 equal portions.

Get three shallow bowls ready, the first holding the plain/all-purpose flour seasoned with salt and pepper, the next with a whole egg beaten with the milk and the last bowl filled with the breadcrumbs.

Take a portion of sausage meat and make a patty with it in your palm. Place a quail's egg in the centre and gently mould the sausage meat around it before rolling it into a ball between your palms. Repeat with the rest of the sausage meat and quails' eggs. Roll each scotch egg firstly in seasoned flour, then dip it in the beaten egg and milk before coating it in the breadcrumbs.

Preheat the oil in a deep fat fryer or large heavy-based saucepan to 180°C (350°F). When a cube of bread dropped in sizzles, browns and rises to the surface, then it should be ready.

Fry a few eggs at a time for about 4 minutes until they are golden brown all over. Remove with a slotted spoon and transfer to a plate lined with kitchen paper to soak up any excess oil. Leave to cool before serving.

120 g/1 cup plain/all-purpose flour, plus extra for dusting

250 ml/1 cup India pale ale

2 large brown onions

vegetable oil, for frying

salt

Tomato Ketchup (see page 125), to serve

serves 4

Onion rings and French fries often compete for the title of most-wanted side dish in a pub. Although French fries are more common, it isn't until you have a home-made onion ring in your mouth that you realize that if you were given the option, you would choose onion rings all day. This batter includes India pale ale (IPA), which adds a lovely richness. The alcohol cooks off when the onions are fried.

ale-battered onion rings

Put the flour into a mixing bowl and make a well in the centre. Pour the ale into the well and whisk until combined. Let the mixture rest, covered for 1 hour.

Peel the onions and cut them crosswise into 1-cm/½-inch thick rings. Dust the rings with more flour, shaking off the excess.

Heat 5 cm/2 inches of vegetable oil in a large, heavy-based frying pan/skillet. The pan is at the right temperature when the oil is steadily bubbling.

Working in batches, dip the onion rings into the batter, then lower into the hot oil and fry until they're golden in colour, turning them over halfway through.

Use a slotted spoon to transfer the onion rings to kitchen paper to drain the excess oil. Sprinkle them with salt and serve with homemade tomato ketchup.

2 slices of white bread

1 heaped teaspoon smoked paprika

30 g/½ cup grated Parmesan cheese

plain/all-purpose flour, for dredging

1 egg, lightly beaten

vegetable oil, for frying

500 g/1 lb. plaice fillets, skinned and sliced into finger-sized portions

salt

tartare sauce

100 ml/scant ½ cup mayonnaise

½ red onion, peeled and finely diced

1 teaspoon Dijon mustard

1½ tablespoons capers

1½ tablespoons cornichons, thinly sliced

serves 4

Crispy breadcrumbed goujons served with a moreish dipping sauce are a classic pub snack. These ones are made with plaice as the base, which makes for a tasty change from the norm. You could also use chicken if you prefer, though, and just cook them for a little longer and serve with barbecue sauce instead.

plaice goujons with tartare sauce

Preheat the oven to 180°C (350°F) Gas 4.

Make the tartare sauce by mixing all of the ingredients together. Set aside in the fridge until needed.

To make the breadcrumbs for the fish fingers, put the bread slices directly onto the shelf of the preheated oven and bake for 5 minutes until crisp and golden. Leave to cool, then place the bread in a resealable bag. Crush to coarse breadcrumbs using a rolling pin. Add a generous pinch of salt, the paprika and Parmesan, reseal the bag and shake to combine.

Transfer the breadcrumbs to a large plate. Put the flour and beaten egg on separate plates.

Pour a little oil (about 2-mm/1/16-inch deep) in a large frying pan/skillet and set over a medium heat. Dredge the plaice portions in the flour, shaking off the excess, then coat in the egg and finally the breadcrumbs before carefully placing in the pan.

Cook the fish fingers for 1 minute on each side, or until golden brown and the fish is cooked through. Drain the excess oil on kitchen paper and then serve immediately with the tartare sauce for dipping.

1 x 250-g/9-oz. Camembert

2 sprigs of fresh thyme, leaves only

2 tablespoons runny honey

to serve

1 red (bell) pepper, deseeded and sliced into 1-cm/½-inch thick pieces

1 Granny Smith apple, cored and sliced into 8 wedges

1 large carrot, peeled and cut into 3-cm/1¼-inch fingers

sliced sourdough bread

serves 2–4

How to make friends and influence people? Serve them this oozing, melted cheese with a selection of colourful chopped vegetables and apple slices. Add a glass of red to the equation and you'll be everyone's favourite for life.

baked honey and thyme Camembert with crudités

Preheat the oven to 200°C (400°F) Gas 6.

Score the top of the Camembert in a cross-hatch pattern with a sharp knife, but leave the cheese in the box.

Push the thyme leaves into the scores, then drizzle over the honey. Replace the lid, loosely, and place the box on a baking sheet.

Bake the Camembert in the preheated oven for 20 minutes until the cheese is all melted and wobbles when you move the pan gently.

Serve the Camembert with the (bell) pepper, apple and carrot crudités and sliced sourdough bread.

500 g/1 lb. diced beef

160 g/5½ oz. swede/rutabaga, finely diced

160 g/5½ oz. carrot, peeled and finely diced

75 g/2½ oz. onion, finely diced

½ sprig of fresh thyme, leaves only

salt and freshly ground black pepper

butter, for greasing

for the pastry

500 g/1 lb. butter

1 kg/2 lb. 4 oz. plain/all-purpose flour, plus extra for dusting

cold water, to bind

1 egg, lightly beaten, to glaze

25-cm/10-inch pastry/cookie cutter

makes 6 large pasties

A traditional Cornish pasty is a thing of beauty! They are easy to demolish in one quick sitting and not as tricky to make as people think. It's a good recipe to have in your repertoire.

Cornish pasties

Preheat the oven to 180°C (350°F) Gas 4.

Make the pastry first by crumbling the butter and flour, plus some salt and pepper together with your fingertips. Then add a little cold water, just a splash at a time, until the pastry comes together.

Sprinkle a little more flour over a work surface and use a rolling pin to roll out the pastry to a thickness of about 5 mm/¼ inch. Use the cutter to cut out six 25-cm/10-inch circles. Either leave the circles out if you've got space on your work surface or stack them up with a little baking parchment in between to keep them separate.

Put the beef, swede/rutabaga, carrot, onion, thyme and some salt and pepper in a bowl and mix well. Divide the filling among the pastry circles and spread it out evenly on the right side of each circle, so that you can fold over the other side. Pull the left side over and press it together to seal 1 cm/½ inch away from the edge of the right hand side of the pastry. This allows a little room to fold the edge back over the fold to seal in the filling nice and tightly.

Lay some baking parchment on a baking sheet (you can grease this a little with some butter, too, to be safe), slide a palette knife/metal spatula under the pasties and lift them carefully onto the paper. Bake in the preheated oven for 45 minutes and serve straight away or chill in the fridge for up to a week.

Pastry Tip: You can also wrap the uncooked pastries and filling in clingfilm/plastic wrap or foil and freeze them for up to 3 months, as long as the meat hasn't been previously frozen. It's a really handy thing to have ready in the freezer and bakes perfectly well from frozen in a preheated oven at 160°C (325°F) Gas 3 for 90 minutes.

6 oysters, shucked

1 tablespoon crème fraîche or double/heavy cream

1 tablespoon dry white wine

1 tablespoon grated lemon zest

2 tablespoons shaved fennel

1 teaspoon fennel fronds

1 tablespoon flaked/slivered almonds, toasted

freshly ground black pepper

sourdough bread and butter, to serve

steamer with a lid

serves 2

The famous food of love – this sexy snack is for the more sophisticated among you. If you feel like serving up something special of an evening that takes minimal effort, go for this. Just be sure to get the best quality oysters you can find.

steamed oysters

Pour off some of the oyster's natural juices. Layer the shells so that they stay upright in a steamer basket.

Carefully dot the oysters with crème fraiche or cream, drizzle with white wine and sprinkle over the lemon zest.

Bring the water to a medium simmer and cover the steamer with the lid. Steam the oysters for 5–7 minutes.

Carefully lift out the oysters with a large spoon and transfer to serving plates. Top the oysters with shaved fennel, fennel fronds, toasted almonds and freshly ground black pepper.

Serve with good sourdough bread and butter.

chapter 2

MEATY MAINS

2 large, skinless, chicken breasts

1 teaspoon chopped
fresh tarragon

40 g/5 tablespoons plain/
all-purpose flour

3 eggs, lightly beaten

100 g/2 cups dried breadcrumbs

300 ml/1¼ cups sunflower oil,
for frying

Buttery Crushed Potatoes
(see page 113), to serve

garlic butter

50 g/3½ tablespoons
butter, softened

1 garlic clove, finely chopped

2 big pinches of chopped
fresh parsley

freshly squeezed juice of ¼
lemon (save the rest of the
lemon to serve)

salt and freshly
ground black pepper

serves 2

When buying chicken breasts for this, find the largest and plumpest possible; it will really help with keeping the garlic butter in the middle.

chicken kievs

Start by making the garlic butter. Mix the butter, garlic, parsley and lemon juice in a bowl and season with salt and pepper. Portion the butter into two flat, thin pieces, approximately 2-cm/¾-inch wide and 4 cm/1½ inches long, so that they'll slot into the opening in the chicken breast. Wrap in foil and put in the fridge to harden while you prepare the chicken.

Cut the 'false fillet' off the chicken breasts (the small piece of muscle on the side) and keep to one side as you're going to use these to plug the hole in the side. Lay each breast flat, push down on the top to level it flat and carefully slice through the middle, front to back, so that there's a cut down one side. Don't cut all the way through; the cut needs to go about three quarters of the way through.

Take the garlic butter from the fridge and place a piece inside each breast. Take the false fillets and slot them in after the garlic butter to help 'plug' the cut on each breast.

Mix the tarragon with the flour. Roll each stuffed breast in the seasoned flour, then dip in the egg and finally cover really well with breadcrumbs. Wrap in foil and place in the fridge for 30 minutes.

Take the kievs out of the fridge and repeat the coating process: flour first, then egg and then breadcrumbs.

Preheat the oil in a deep fat fryer or large heavy-based saucepan until a cube of bread browns in 20 seconds. Carefully lower the kievs into the hot oil and fry for 20 minutes, or until cooked through, turning carefully once halfway through cooking.

Remove with a slotted spoon and drain the excess oil on kitchen paper, then serve the kievs with a lemon wedge to squeeze over the top, buttery crushed potatoes and salad leaves, if you like.

2 bone-in lamb shanks

20 g/1½ tablespoons butter

2 garlic cloves, roughly chopped

1 lemon, halved

4–6 fresh mint leaves

salt and freshly ground
black pepper

Buttery Crushed Potatoes
(see page 113), to serve

Red Wine Gravy
(see page 122), to serve

serves 2

Melt-in-the-mouth lamb shank is popular pub grub, probably partly because it presents really well on the plate and looks very cool. However, it's actually very simple to cook at home. Served with Buttery Crushed Potatoes (see page 122), it is just heaven.

slow-cooked lamb shanks

Preheat the oven to 190°C (375°F) Gas 5.

Fold a large piece of foil in half to make it double-strength and place it in a roasting pan. You're going to need enough foil either side to cover and seal the lamb shanks inside.

Sit the lamb shanks on their flat ends on the tin foil and rub with butter all over. Add the garlic, lemon and mint leaves. Season well with salt and pepper.

Keeping the foil open at this stage, place the meat in the oven and roast for 10 minutes, then fold in all the sides of the foil so that the shanks are sealed inside and fully covered. Reduce the oven temperature to 160°C (325°F) Gas 3 and cook for 1 hour.

Remove the foil and prod the meat with a fork. If it feels tender and looks like it's falling off the bone then it's ready. If it still resists the pressure of the fork, you might have a bigger shank that needs another 15 minutes or so. Once it's tender, open up the foil and turn up the temperature again to 190°C (375°F) Gas 5. Pop the lamb shanks back in the oven for 5 minutes to brown and crisp a little.

Spoon the meat juices over the shanks and then put them on serving plates. Serve with buttery crushed potatoes and red wine gravy.

4 tablespoons olive oil

1.5–2 kg/3¼–4½ lb. beef short ribs, trimmed if very fatty

75 g/2½ oz. (approx. 5 slices) prosciutto, finely chopped

1 large onion, finely chopped

2 carrots, peeled and finely chopped

2 celery stalks, finely chopped

3 garlic cloves, finely chopped

1 bottle of medium quality full-bodied red wine

1 large tablespoon double concentrated tomato purée/paste

3 anchovies in oil, drained

1 large strip of orange peel

500 ml/2 cups good quality beef stock/broth

1 sprig of fresh rosemary

1 sprig of fresh thyme

2 bay leaves

1 dried chipotle chilli (deseeded or with half the seeds left in if you like it hot)

salt and freshly ground black pepper

Creamy Mashed Potatoes (see page 110), to serve

serves 6–8

The smoky chipotle and aromatic orange zest give this traditional bourguignon base a little extra pizazz. Serve with mashed potatoes for ultimate enjoyment.

beef short ribs

Preheat the oven to 160°C (325°F) Gas 3.

Heat the oil over a medium-high heat in a large heavy-based ovenproof saucepan with a lid. Add the ribs and brown on all sides. Once well-browned, remove the ribs, set aside and season.

Reduce the heat to medium-low and, in the same pan, sauté the prosciutto until it begins to crisp.

Add the onion, carrots, celery and garlic and cook until the vegetables are softened. Deglaze the pan with one glass of wine, scraping the bottom of the pan with a wooden spoon to make sure that you incorporate all the caramelized cooking juices.

When the wine has almost evaporated, add the rest of the wine, tomato purée/paste, anchovies, orange peel, stock/broth, rosemary, thyme, bay leaves and chipotle chilli.

Stir well and add the ribs back to the pan along with any juices. Bring to the boil, then transfer to the preheated oven with the lid tightly on, and cook for 2½ hours, or until the meat is tender. Turn the ribs occasionally during cooking to make sure all sides get immersed in the sauce. If at the end of cooking, your sauce is too thin, remove the meat and reduce the sauce over a low heat until thickened.

Remove the rosemary, thyme and bay leaf and serve the short ribs with the sauce from the cooking pan and creamy mashed potatoes.

600 g/1 lb 5 oz. venison
sausages

2 tablespoons olive oil

braised red cabbage

1 onion, halved and sliced

2 tablespoons olive oil,
plus extra if needed

800 g/about 8 cups thinly sliced
red cabbage

½ teaspoon ground cinnamon

½ teaspoon ground allspice

1 kg/2 lb 4 oz. tart eating
apples, peeled, cored and
chopped

75g/⅓ cup plus
2 tablespoons raisins

200 g/2 cups chestnuts
(optional)

250 ml/1 cup apple juice,
plus extra if needed

200 ml/¾ cup passata/strained
tomatoes

1–2 tablespoons cider vinegar

a pinch of sugar (optional)

salt and freshly ground
black pepper

Red Wine Gravy
(see page 122), to serve

Creamy Mashed Potatoes
(see page 110), to serve

serves 4

This is real comfort food, poshed up for a dinner party.
Red cabbage goes well with sausages and any kind of
potato dish. The taste improves with time so this is a
good dish to make in advance. Easy to make. Everyone
will love it. Win, win!

venison sausages with braised red cabbage and red wine gravy

For the red cabbage, put the onion and oil in a frying pan/skillet
with a lid and cook for about 3 minutes until soft. Add the cabbage,
spices, apples and raisins and more oil if needed. Toss together and
cook for 2–3 minutes. Stir in the chestnuts (if using) and season with
salt and pepper. Add the apple juice, passata/strained tomatoes and
1 tablespoon of the vinegar. Mix well and bring to a simmer. Cover
and simmer gently for about 30 minutes, until the cabbage is tender.

Add more apple juice if the mixture is dry and simmer for a further
15 minutes. Taste and add the remaining vinegar or a little sugar if
needed. Cover the pan and keep warm over a low heat until you are
ready to serve.

Meanwhile, prepare the red wine gravy (see page 122) and mash
(see page 110).

Add the oil to a separate frying pan/skillet and brown the sausages
well on all sides. Drain off the fat and add the sausages to the gravy
in the pan. Leave over a low heat for 10 minutes for the sausages to
finish cooking and absorb some of the flavour.

Serve the sausages and gravy with the red cabbage and creamy
mashed potatoes.

220 g/8 oz. lean minced/
ground beef

2 teaspoons tomato purée/paste

1½ tablespoons fresh
breadcrumbs

1 teaspoon chopped
fresh parsley

1 tablespoon olive oil

salt and freshly ground
black pepper

to serve

2 sesame seeded burger buns

Tomato Ketchup (see page 125)

6 lettuce leaves

Triple-cooked Fries
(see page 108)

makes 2 burgers

If you're ever not sure what to make, but you know you fancy something casual, delicious and just a tad indulgent – it has to be burgers all the way. This classic combination of meat patty, bun, fries and tomato ketchup is a tale as old as time. A bit of lettuce never hurt anyone, either. Those salad dodgers can take it out if they wish.

classic beef burgers with tomato ketchup and lettuce

Put the beef in a bowl with the tomato purée/paste, breadcrumbs, parsley and some salt and pepper. Work together with your hands until evenly mixed. Divide the beef mixture in half and shape it into two burger patties. Press each burger down to make it nice and flat.

Heat the oil in a frying pan/skillet and fry the burgers over medium-high heat for 5 minutes on each side until cooked through.

Slice the burger buns in half. Spread a spoonful of tomato ketchup on the base of each bun and put the cooked burgers on top. Put a few lettuce leaves on top of each burger and finish with the lids of the buns. Serve with triple cooked fries.

1 tablespoon vegetable oil

1 bay leaf

1 onion, finely chopped

1 celery stalk, finely chopped

½ carrot, peeled and finely chopped

500 g/1 lb. lean minced/ground beef

150 g/5 oz. white/cup and button mushrooms, chopped

a splash of dry white wine (optional)

3 tablespoons tomato purée/paste

100 ml/scant ½ cup beef or chicken stock/broth

900 g/2 lb. fluffy/Idaho potatoes, peeled and cut into chunks

2 teaspoons butter

2 tablespoons double/heavy cream

½ teaspoon truffle oil

3 tablespoons grated Cheddar cheese

1 tablespoon grated Parmesan cheese

salt and freshly ground black pepper

serves 4

Cottage pie goes upmarket! Using a touch of truffle oil to flavour the mashed potato is a simple but effective way to give a new dimension to this homely dish. Adding mushrooms to the meat mixture brings texture as well as flavour. Bake until golden brown and serve it straight from the oven, accompanied by veggies, for a soul-soothing meal.

truffled mash cottage pie

Preheat the oven to 200°C (400°F) Gas 6.

Heat the oil in a large frying pan/skillet over a medium heat. Add the bay leaf, onion, celery and carrot and fry, stirring, until the onion is softened. Add the beef and fry until browned, stirring often.

Add the mushrooms and fry for 3 minutes. Pour in the white wine (if using) and fry briefly until cooked off. Mix in the tomato purée/paste and the stock/broth. Season with salt and freshly ground black pepper. Simmer for 10–15 minutes, stirring often.

Meanwhile, cook the potatoes in a large pan of salted, boiling water until tender; about 20 minutes. Drain, then mash with butter, cream and truffle oil and season with salt and freshly ground black pepper.

Place the beef mixture in an ovenproof dish. Top with the mashed potato, spreading in an even layer. Sprinkle over the Cheddar and Parmesan cheese.

Bake in the preheated oven for 30 minutes until golden brown. Serve hot from the oven.

600 g/1 lb 5 oz. all-purpose potatoes, such as Maris Piper or Yukon Gold, peeled and chopped into 2-cm/¾-inch chunks

45 g/3 tablespoons butter

1 garlic clove, finely chopped

2 carrots, chopped

1 white onion, chopped

500 g/1 lb. minced/ground lamb

20 g/4 teaspoons tomato purée/paste

200 ml/scant 1 cup red wine

150 ml/⅔ cup vegetable stock/broth

a pinch of dried rosemary

a pinch of dried thyme

40 g/generous ⅓ cup old fashioned/rolled oats

50 ml/3½ tablespoons full-fat/whole milk

20 g/⅓ cup finely grated Parmesan, plus extra for sprinkling on top (optional)

salt and freshly ground black pepper

serves 4

Shepherd's pie uses lamb mince, whereas cottage pie uses beef mince – this comforting pie is lovely with either, really, so use what you have to hand. The porridge oats seem a bit unorthodox but they help to make the mixture soft and tender.

shepherd's pie

Preheat the oven to 180°C (350°F) Gas 4.

Cook the potatoes in a large pan of salted, boiling water until tender; about 20 minutes.

Meanwhile, heat 15 g/1 tablespoon of the butter in a frying pan/skillet over a medium heat and add the garlic, carrots and onion. Fry for about 4–5 minutes, until softened and starting to brown. Add the lamb and fry until cooked, breaking it up as it cooks with a spoon.

Add the tomato purée/paste and stir in. Then add the red wine, vegetable stock/broth, rosemary, thyme and some salt and pepper. Stir well and then add the oats, a little at a time. Mix well and cook, stirring, until the mixture is nice and thick and the oats have absorbed the liquid.

By now the potatoes should be soft, so drain and mash them, mixing in the milk, Parmesan and remaining 30 g/2 tablespoons of the butter.

Spoon the lamb mixture into a greased ovenproof dish and press down to make it level. Spread the potatoes over the top evenly.

Put the dish in the preheated oven and bake for 20 minutes. To brown the top, add a little more Parmesan (or sprinkle with grated mature Cheddar) and place under a hot grill/broiler for the last 5 minutes.

2 tablespoons lard or goose fat or vegetable or sunflower oil

8 thick-cut lamb chops

2 turnips, peeled and chopped into chunks

2 carrots, peeled, halved lengthways and cut into 2.5-cm/1-inch pieces

2 leeks, thinly sliced

1 tablespoon chopped fresh parsley, plus extra to garnish

450 g/15¾ oz. potatoes, peeled and very thinly sliced

600 ml/2½ cups lamb, beef or chicken stock/broth

25 g/1½ tablespoons butter, melted

salt and freshly ground black pepper

serves 4

A much-loved regional classic of British cuisine, this hearty dish makes an excellent Sunday lunch. The slow-cooked combination of succulent lamb meat and soft, stock-soaked potatoes is truly tasty.

Lancashire hotpot

Preheat the oven to 200°C (400°F) Gas 6.

Heat the lard, goose fat or oil in a large frying pan/skillet. Fry the lamb chops until lightly browned on both sides and then season with salt and freshly ground black pepper. Remove from the heat.

Layer the ingredients in a heavy-based casserole dish, seasoning each layer with salt and freshly ground black pepper as you do so, as follows: first, place half the turnips, carrots and leeks in the bottom of the dish. Top with the lamp chops, sprinkling them with the parsley. Layer with the remaining turnips, carrots and leeks. Layer the potato slices over the vegetables, overlapping the slices.

Pour the stock/broth into the casserole dish and, on the hob/stovetop, bring to the boil.

Brush the potato topping with the melted butter. Cover the casserole and bake in the preheated oven for 1¾ hours. Uncover the casserole and bake for a further 15 minutes until the potatoes are golden. Garnish with parsley and serve.

15 g/½ oz. dried porcini mushrooms

2 tablespoons olive oil

1 onion, finely chopped

1 celery stalk, finely chopped

½ carrot, peeled and finely chopped

2 fresh sage leaves, shredded

1 sprig of fresh rosemary, leaves only, finely chopped

200 g/6½ oz. white/cup mushrooms, finely chopped

500 g/1 lb. minced/ ground beef

1 garlic clove, finely chopped

100 ml/scant ½ cup red wine

500 g/2 cups passata/ strained tomatoes

200 ml/1 scant cup beef stock/broth

50 g/3 tablespoons butter

6 tablespoons plain/ all-purpose flour

600 ml/2½ cups full-fat/ whole milk

3 tablespoons double/ heavy cream

1 teaspoon truffle oil

9–12 dried lasagne sheets

50 g/⅔ cup grated Parmesan cheese

salt and freshly ground black pepper

serves 6

A rich, even more indulgent take on classic lasagne, this is ideal for entertaining as it can be made in advance; serve it simply with salad and garlic bread on the side. Bliss.

truffled mushroom lasagna

Soak the dried porcini in hot water for 20 minutes; drain and chop.

To make the meat sauce, heat the olive oil in a casserole dish over a medium heat. Add the onion, celery, carrot, sage and rosemary and fry, stirring, for 2–3 minutes, until the onion has softened. Add the porcini and white/cup mushrooms and cook, stirring, for 2 minutes. Add the beef and fry until browned on all sides. Sprinkle in the garlic and add the red wine. Cook, stirring, for 2–3 minutes until the red wine has largely reduced. Add the passata/strained tomatoes and beef stock/broth. Season with salt and freshly ground black pepper. Bring to the boil, then reduce the heat and simmer uncovered for 1 hour, stirring occasionally, until the sauce is thickened and reduced.

Meanwhile, make the white sauce. Melt the butter in a heavy-based saucepan. Add the flour and cook, stirring, for 2 minutes. Gradually add the milk, stirring well with each addition to ensure that there are no lumps. Season with salt and freshly ground black pepper. Bring to the boil, while stirring, until the sauce thickens. Stir in the cream and the truffle oil. Set aside.

Preheat the oven to 200°C (400°F) Gas 6.

In a baking dish, place a spoonful of the meat sauce, spreading it thinly over the base. Add a layer of lasagne sheets. Top with another layer of the meat sauce, then spread 1–2 tablespoons of the truffled white sauce over the meat. Sprinkle with a little Parmesan. Repeat the layering process, finishing with a generous layer of the white sauce and topping with the remaining Parmesan. Bake the lasagne in the preheated oven for 40 minutes, until golden brown. Serve.

115 g/¾ cup plus 2 tbsp plain/
all-purpose flour

2 UK large/US extra-large eggs

250 ml/1 cup full-fat/whole milk

a small bunch of fresh
chives, snipped into 3 cm/1¼
inch pieces

12 tiny chipolata sausages or
cocktail sausages, or 6 larger
sausages cut in half

1 eating apple, such as
a Bramley, unpeeled, cored, cut
into slices 12 slices (optional)

4 tablespoons vegetable oil

salt and freshly ground black
pepper

Creamy Mashed Potatoes (see
page 110), to serve

1 or 2 large muffin tins

makes 12 individual toads:
serves 4 to 6

This adored British staple of sausages cooked in Yorkshire pudding batter is taken up a notch with the addition of tangy apple. Good quality sausages make all the difference here.

toad in the hole

Adjust the oven shelves – you will be using the middle one for the muffin tin, so make sure there is plenty of room for the batter to rise above the tin. Put a shelf under the middle one and put a large roasting pan on it to catch any drips.

Preheat the oven to 220°C (425°F) Gas 7.

To make the batter, put the flour and some salt and pepper in a large bowl. Make a hollow in the centre, then break the eggs into the hollow. Pour the milk into the hollow.

Using a balloon whisk, mix the eggs with the milk. Start to mix the flour into the hollow. When all the flour has been mixed in, whisk the batter well to get rid of any lumps. Add the snipped chives and whisk them into the batter.

Using kitchen scissors, snip the links between the sausages.

Put 1 teaspoon of oil into each hole of the muffin tin, then put it into the oven to heat. Carefully remove the pan after 5 minutes – the oil will be very hot – and put it on a heatproof work surface. Put one chipolata or half a large sausage in each hole, plus a slice of apple, if using, then put the tin back in the oven for 5 minutes.

Pour or ladle the batter into a large jug and stir it.

Carefully remove the hot tin and pour the batter into each hole so each one is half full. Bake for 20 minutes until golden brown.

Remove from the oven and ease each toad out of its hole with a knife. Eat straight away with creamy mashed potatoes.

75 g/⅔ cup plain/all-purpose flour, sifted

a pinch of salt

3 eggs

100 ml/scant ½ cup full-fat/whole milk

butter, for frying

2 tablespoons olive oil

1 banana shallot, finely chopped

250 g/8 oz. field mushrooms, finely chopped

250 g/8 oz. chestnut/cremini mushrooms, finely chopped

15 g/½ oz. dried porcini mushrooms, soaked in hot water for 20 minutes, then squeezed dry, chopped

grated fresh nutmeg

700 g/1½ lb. piece of beef fillet of even thickness

1 tablespoon Dijon or wholegrain mustard

300 g/10 oz. ready-made puff pastry

1 egg, lightly beaten, to glaze

salt and freshly ground black pepper

25-cm/10-inch frying pan/skilllet

serves 6

This iconic dish requires a fair bit of preparation. However, it looks and tastes magnificent.

beef wellington

Stir together the flour and salt in a mixing bowl. Make a well in the centre and break the eggs in. Gradually whisk in the milk to form a batter. Heat a knob/pat of butter in the 25-cm/10-inch frying pan/skillet over a medium heat. Pour in a quarter of the batter, tilting the pan to spread it evenly. Fry the pancake until set, then flip over to brown the other side. Repeat to make four pancakes in total. Cool.

Heat 1 tablespoon of olive oil in a large, heavy frying pan/skillet. Add the shallot and fry over a low heat for 3 minutes, stirring, until softened. Add the mushrooms. Season with salt, pepper and nutmeg. Fry, stirring, for 20 minutes until the mixture is dry. Turn into a colander. Leave to cool, then cover and chill for 1 hour.

Season the beef with salt and pepper. Heat the remaining oil in a large frying pan/skillet over a high heat. Add the beef and brown on all sides. Set aside to cool, wrap and chill for 1 hour.

Put a large rectangle of clingfilm/plastic wrap on a work surface. Place the pancakes on top, overlapping the edges to form a rough 'rectangle', large enough to encase the beef. Spread the mushroom mixture over the pancakes. Brush the beef with the mustard. Place the beef in the centre of the pancakes and use the plastic to roll into a parcel. Twist the plastic ends together and chill for 30 minutes.

Roll out the pastry on a lightly floured work surface to form two big rectangles, one slightly larger. Unwrap the beef and put in the centre of the smaller rectangle. Brush the edges of the pastry with beaten egg. Cover the beef with the other rectangle, pressing the edges together with a fork. Trim to form a neat parcel. Chill for 30 minutes.

Preheat the oven to 200°C (400°F) Gas 6. Place the wellington on a baking sheet and brush with beaten egg. Bake in the preheated oven for 40 minutes until golden. Stand for 10 minutes before serving.

20 g/1½ tablespoons butter, plus extra if needed

750 g/1 lb 10 oz. diced beef

250 g/9 oz. beef or lamb's kidneys, diced

2 white onions, chopped

3 carrots, peeled and chopped

60 g/1 cup white/cup mushrooms, chopped

1½ tablespoons plain/all-purpose flour

a pinch of chopped fresh thyme leaves

a pinch of chopped fresh sage

4 teaspoons tomato purée/paste

2 teaspoons Worcestershire sauce

800 ml/3⅓ cups beef stock/broth, plus extra if needed

plain/all-purpose flour, for dusting

300 g/10 oz. ready-made puff pastry

1 egg, lightly beaten, to glaze

salt and freshly ground black pepper

20-cm/8-inch round pie dish

pie funnel (optional)

serves 4

Another traditional meat dish that is still popular because it is just so tasty. Serve with peas and a glass of smooth ale on the side.

steak and kidney pie

Melt the butter in a frying pan/skillet over a medium heat and set a large saucepan on another burner over a medium heat. Brown the diced beef first in the frying/pan, in batches, and add it to the saucepan as soon as is it sealed. Do the same with the diced kidneys – no need to cook these through yet, it's just browning for flavour.

Add the onion, carrots and mushrooms to the frying pan/skillet, with a little more butter if needed, and fry for a few minutes until softened. Tip the vegetables into the saucepan and stir. Sprinkle the flour on top – don't stir again until the flour starts to change colour. Stir in the thyme, sage, tomato purée/paste and Worcestershire Sauce and season with salt and pepper. Pour in the beef stock/broth and bring to the boil, then reduce the heat to a low simmer and cook for up to 2 hours, with the lid half-on. It might be thick enough after 90 minutes, so check and stir occasionally. Add more stock/broth if it's too thick. If it's too thin, remove the lid and increase the heat a little.

Preheat the oven to 180°C (350°F) Gas 4.

Roll out the pastry on a lightly floured work surface until big enough to generously cover your pie dish. If you have a pie funnel, put this in the centre of the dish. Pour the filling mixture into the pie dish and place the pastry on top. Cut a small cross in the centre of the pastry (directly on top of the pie funnel, if using, so steam can escape). Trim the edges or let them overhang as you prefer, and press around the edge of the pie lid to seal it to the sides of the pie. Brush the pastry with beaten egg. Transfer the dish to a baking sheet and bake in the preheated oven for 30–40 minutes, until the top is golden brown.

25 g/2 tablespoons butter

1 onion, finely chopped

25 g/3 tablespoons plain/
all-purpose flour

400 ml/1⅔ cups chicken stock/
broth

2 tablespoons double/
heavy cream

25 g/4–5 sprigs of fresh parsley,
finely chopped

1 tablespoon olive oil

300 g/10 oz. button
mushrooms, halved

700 g/1½ lb. cooked chicken,
chopped into large chunks

150 g/1 cup cooked peas

250 g/8 oz. ready-made
shortcrust pastry

1 egg, lightly beaten, to glaze

salt and freshly ground
black pepper

23-cm/9-inch round pie dish

serves 6

With its creamy-textured sauce and satisfying filling, this is soothing comfort food at its best. Serve it for Sunday lunch, accompanied by boiled new potatoes, broccoli and glazed carrots.

chicken and mushroom pie

To make the sauce, melt the butter in a heavy-based saucepan. Add the onion and cook over a medium-low heat until softened but not coloured. Mix in the flour and cook, stirring, for a minute. Gradually, add the stock/broth, stirring as you do so to avoid lumps. Bring to the boil, stirring often, until thickened. Mix in the cream and parsley. Season with salt and freshly ground black pepper. Set aside.

Heat the olive oil in a large frying pan/skillet. Fry the mushrooms over a medium heat until lightly browned. Set aside.

In the pie dish, mix together the cooked chicken, peas and mushrooms. Stir through the sauce and set aside to cool.

Preheat the oven to 200°C (400°F) Gas 6.

Roll out the pastry on a lightly floured work surface. Cover the pie mixture with the pastry lid, using the pastry trimmings to decorate it to your liking. Cut a hole in the centre of the crust to let steam escape. Brush the pastry with beaten egg. Bake in the preheated oven for 1 hour until the pastry is golden brown. Serve hot from the oven.

750 ml/3 cups chicken stock/broth

1 onion, finely diced

3 garlic cloves, finely chopped

2 tablespoons olive oil

200 g/1 cup pearl barley

100 ml/scant ½ cup white wine

400 g/14 oz. skinless, boneless chicken thighs, cut into small chunks

20 g/½ cup finely chopped fresh flat-leaf parsley

2 tablespoons double/heavy cream or crème fraîche

grated zest of ½ lemon

salt and freshly ground black pepper

serves 4

A hearty dinner time treat, the earthy flavour of pearl barley here is complemented by rich cream and fresh parsley and lemon zest. This risotto would be equally delicious with a pint of beer or a chilled glass of white wine, so take your pick.

chicken and parsley pearl barley risotto

Put the stock/broth in a large saucepan and bring to a simmer.

Meanwhile, sauté the onions and the garlic in a casserole dish with the olive oil for 5 minutes until translucent.

Add the pearl barley and stir it all around to mix and mingle. Add the white wine to the pan and cook, stirring, until the wine has reduced by half. Add 2 ladles of the hot stock/broth to the pan. Cook while stirring for 5 minutes.

Add the rest of the stock/broth to the barley along with the chicken and half the parsley. Keep it on a medium-low heat and let it gently bubble away, uncovered, for around 45 minutes, until all the stock/broth has been absorbed into the barley. You don't need to stir constantly, just check on it every now and again.

When the barley has puffed open and the stock/broth has been absorbed, stir in the cream and divide the risotto between serving bowls. Top with the remaining parsley and the lemon zest. Season with salt and pepper and serve.

3 onions, quartered

1 sprig of fresh rosemary

1 small handful of dried mushrooms, such as shiitake

1 x 1.5 kg/3¼ lb. chicken, patted dry with kitchen paper

6 tablespoons olive oil

300 ml/1¼ cups red wine

salt and freshly ground black pepper

super-savoury paste

1 chicken stock/bouillon cube

3 large garlic cloves

4 sun-dried tomatoes

1½ tablespoons olive oil

1 tablespoon maple syrup

½ tablespoon tomato purée/paste

½ tablespoon soy sauce

½ tablespoon fish sauce

1½ tablespoons paprika

½ teaspoon chilli/hot red pepper flakes

2 sprigs of fresh rosemary, leaves only, plus extra for garnishing

You will be hard-pushed to find a better roast chicken recipe than this. To save time, you can make the paste in advance and store it in the fridge for up to three days. Serve the chicken with classic roast potatoes or cheesy polenta for a little something different.

best-ever roast chicken

Preheat the oven to 200°C (400°F) Gas 6.

Place 2 onion quarters, the sprig of rosemary and the dried mushrooms into the cavity of the chicken.

Take the remaining onion quarters and place in a roasting pan to form a trivet (three pronged stand) and place the chicken on top.

Rub the chicken all over with the olive oil and pour any extra in to the tray – this is necessary to create a robust gravy. Season with a sprinkling of salt and plenty of freshly ground black pepper. Place in the preheated oven, uncovered, for 20 minutes.

Meanwhile, make the paste by putting all the ingredients into a food processor and blending until smooth.

Mix the paste with the wine and 300 ml/1¼ cups water.

After 20 minutes, reduce the oven temperature to 180°C (350°F) Gas 4. Remove the roasting pan and pour the paste and wine mixture around the chicken – it is important you don't pour it over the chicken at this stage. Put back into the oven for 50 minutes.

Take the chicken out of the oven and carefully baste it with the rich gravy from the roasting tray, spooning it all over the chicken and into every crevice.

Place back in the oven for a final 15 minutes so that the skin takes on all the flavour of the sauce. Ensure the chicken is cooked by inserting a skewer between the leg and breast. If the juices run clear, then it is cooked. Serve with the gravy from the roasting pan and accompaniments of your choosing. Garnish with extra rosemary.

chapter 3

FISH DISHES

4 smoked mackerel fillets (each about 100 g/3½ oz.), deboned

freshly squeezed juice of ½ lemon

50 ml/3½ tablespoons double/heavy cream

Tabasco, to taste

1 teaspoon horseradish sauce

1 spring onion/scallion, sliced

100 ml/7 tablespoons butter

salt and freshly ground black pepper

to serve

16–20 melba toasts

seeds from 1 pomegranate

a large handful of fresh rocket/arugula

4 ramekins

serves 4

Pretend your kitchen table is a gastro pub with this dinner-party worthy dish. It can be made in advance for ease and the smokiness of the fish combined with the heat of Tabasco is addictive. This recipe uses a fork to create a coarse texture, but you can use a food processor to achieve a smoother finish, or turn it into a pâté if you prefer.

potted smoked mackerel

Place all of the ingredients, except the butter, in a large mixing bowl. Season with salt and pepper, then use a fork to mix and mash everything together. Press the mixture into ramekins and set aside.

Melt the butter in a saucepan set over a medium heat. Spoon the butter over the top of the mackerel while it is still warm. This will form a light seal. Set aside to cool before chilling in the fridge for at least 30 minutes.

Serve the mackerel with melba toasts, pomegranate seeds and some rocket/arugula.

200 g/1⅔ cups plain/
all-purpose flour

1 egg, plus 1 egg yolk

200 g/¾ cup full-fat/whole milk

150 g/5 oz. whitebait/smelt
(or micro-fry whitebait)

15 g/1 tablespoon butter

salt and freshly ground
black pepper

vegetable oil, for frying

mayonnaise, to serve

½ lemon, cut into
wedges, to serve

serves 2

This delicacy is a regular fixture on the menu in many decent pubs. 'Whitebait' refers to the micro-fry of several small species of fish, herrings and sprats being the more common types. In the United Kingdom, whitebait are larger but still served whole. This recipe gives the option for whichever version of the fish you can get your hands on.

crispy whitebait

Sift the flour into a large mixing bowl and add the egg and egg yolk. Stir well, then slowly add all of the milk, stirring as you do – you should end up with a thick batter. Add a generous pinch of salt and black pepper and mix through. Now add the whitebait and carefully fold them through the mixture.

Put the butter and enough vegetable oil to just cover the base in a frying pan/skillet. Set over a medium heat until the butter is foaming.

If the whitebait are larger than micro-fry (as pictured), carefully place the battered whitebait in the pan and cook for 3–4 minutes until golden brown, turning once.

If you are using micro-fry, using a serving spoon, scoop a portion of the whitebait batter mixture into the pan. Cook for 2–3 minutes until golden brown on one side, then flip the whitebait and cook on the other side until brown and cooked through.

Remove the cooked whitebait from the pan using a slotted spoon and drain the excess oil on kitchen paper. Serve immediately with mayonnaise and lemon wedges for squeezing.

Tip The batter recipe works for all sorts of seafood – mussels, prawns or winkles, for example. Cook them in exactly the same way, just replace whitebait with your choice of seafood.

500 g/1 lb. potatoes, peeled and chopped

2 spring onions/scallions, finely chopped

25 g/1½ tablespoons butter

1 tablespoon full-fat/whole milk

grated fresh nutmeg

500 g/1 lb. cooked skinless salmon fillet, flaked

grated zest of 1 lemon

salt and freshly ground black pepper

vegetable or sunflower oil, for shallow-frying

lemon wedges, to serve

Triple-cooked Fries (see page 108), to serve

coating

1 egg, lightly beaten

200 g/6½ oz. fine matzo meal or dry breadcrumbs

watercress sauce

100 g/3½ oz. watercress, roughly chopped, plus extra to serve

freshly squeezed juice of ½ lemon

4 tablespoons mayonnaise

1 tablespoon dry white wine

1 teaspoon Dijon mustard

serves 4

Home-made fishcakes make an appealing light lunch or dinner. This recipe uses cooked fresh salmon, but you can easily substitute other fish such as smoked haddock or canned tuna to good effect.

salmon fishcakes with watercress sauce

Cook the potatoes in a large saucepan of boiling, salted water until tender; drain. While the potatoes are cooking, fry the spring onions/scallions in the butter until softened.

Add the fried spring onions/scallions with the butter and the milk to the cooked potatoes and mash well. Season with freshly ground black pepper and freshly grated nutmeg and allow to cool.

Make the watercress sauce by blending together the watercress and lemon juice into a purée in a food processor. Mix this into the mayonnaise, then stir in the wine and mustard. Season with salt and freshly ground black pepper. Set aside.

Mix the flaked salmon and lemon zest into the mashed potato mixture. Shape into eight fishcakes. For the coating, dip each fishcake first into the beaten egg to coat on all sides, then coat in the matzo meal or breadcrumbs.

Heat the oil in a large frying pan/skillet and fry the fishcakes for 5 minutes on each side, until golden brown. Serve hot or at room temperature with the watercress sauce, lemon wedges, a handful of watercress and some triple cooked fries.

with cider and samphire

1 brown onion, peeled and finely chopped

1 tablespoon vegetable oil

1 garlic clove, peeled and finely chopped

1 kg/2 lb 4 oz. mussels

300 ml/1¼ cups cider

150 g/5½ oz. samphire

50 ml/3½ tablespoons double/heavy cream

with wine (marinière)

2 red onions, peeled and finely chopped

1 tablespoon vegetable oil

1 garlic clove, peeled and finely chopped

1 kg/2 lb 4 oz. mussels

200 ml/¾ cup white wine mixed with 100 ml/ scant ½ cup water

50 ml/3½ tablespoons double/heavy Cream

with ale and garlic

1 brown onion, peeled and finely chopped

1 tablespoon vegetable oil

3 garlic cloves, peeled and finely chopped

1 kg/2 lb 4 oz. mussels

300 ml/1¼ cups ale

50 ml/3½ tablespoons double/heavy cream

each serves 4

To be honest, mussels work well with most alcoholic drinks, but here are three variations to try. Cider adds a lovely apple sweetness that works well with the mussels and samphire adds a wonderful light, salty flavour; wine is the classic accompaniment and is best served simply with crusty bread; while ale is hearty and the extra garlic adds depth and body to the dish.

mussels three ways

For each recipe, in a large pan set over a gentle heat, sweat off the onion in the vegetable oil until translucent. Add the garlic (the garlic will burn if you add it at the same time as the onion) and continue to cook gently for another couple of minutes.

Meanwhile, prepare the mussels by gently rinsing under cold water and removing any 'beards'. Use a table knife (or any blunt knife) to scrape any loose barnacles off the shells and grab the beard with it to pull it off.

For mussels with cider and samphire, remove any hard stalks from the samphire, then finely chop.

Put all of the mussels into a saucepan set over a high heat, add the alcohol and cover. Bring to the boil for 2–3 minutes until the mussels have opened – don't overboil or you'll have rubbery mussels.

Take off the heat, add the double/heavy cream and samphire (if using), stir and spoon the mussels into big bowls (there's going to be a little grit at the bottom of the pan, so don't serve the last spoonful of the sauce).

Serve with generous hunks of bread to mop-up the delicious juices.

Note: Like most seafood, raw mussels should have no aroma; if they smell overly fishy or of ammonia, don't eat them. Discard any mussels that will not close when tapped gently, before cooking, as well as those which do not open after cooking.

2 cod or haddock fillets, skinned and boned

200 g/1½ cups plain/all-purpose flour

2 teaspoons sea salt

2 x 330 ml/11 fl oz. bottles of lager

sunflower or vegetable oil, for frying

to serve

4 slices of crusty white bread

butter, for spreading

Tartare Sauce (see page 27)

handful of cos/romaine lettuce leaves, cut into strips

Triple-cooked Fries (see page 108)

makes 2 sandwiches

The posh fish finger sandwich is one of London's most famous dishes. Lager is often used in the batter for a richer flavour. Homemade tartare sauce and triple cooked fries finish the meal.

posh fish finger sandwiches

Slice the fish into six finger-size strips in total and set aside.

Whisk the flour, salt and lager in a mixing bowl until combined into a smooth batter.

Fill a large frying pan/skillet with about 2.5 cm/1 inch of oil over a high heat. When the oil is bubbling steadily, it's ready to use. Dip the fish fingers in the batter one by one, shaking off any excess, then lower them carefully into the oil, using tongs if needed. Fry for about 4 minutes on each side over a medium heat until golden and crispy.

Remove the fish fingers carefully from the oil and drain well on kitchen paper.

To assemble the sandwiches, butter the bread before spreading a couple of tablespoons of tartare sauce on top. Place 3 fish fingers each on two slices of bread, then add a few strips of lettuce. Sandwich the other slices of bread on top and serve with triple cooked fries.

vegetable oil, for frying

1 brown onion, peeled
and diced

2 teaspoons garam masala

1 teaspoon turmeric powder

200 g/1½ cup long-grain rice

a pinch of salt

4 hard-boiled/hard-cooked eggs

50 g/⅓ cup frozen peas

2 red chillies/chiles, thinly sliced

a small bunch of fresh
flat-leaf parsley

2 smoked mackerel
fillets, skinned and flaked

50 ml/3½ tablespoons
double/heavy cream

serves 4

Originating in India as a breakfast dish called
'khichdi', kedgeree was brought back to the United
Kingdom in Victorian times and modified as part of the
Anglo-Indian cuisine of the time. This version uses
flavourful smoked mackerel, but you can also try it
with the more traditional smoked haddock.

mackerel kedgeree

Add just enough oil to cover the base of a medium saucepan and set
over a medium heat. Add the onion, garam masala and turmeric and
heat for a couple of minutes before adding the rice. Stir to coat the
rice in the oil and spices, then add 400 ml/1 2/3 cups of water and the
salt. Bring to a simmer, then take the pan off the heat, cover and set
aside to allow the rice to finish cooking for 15 minutes.

Peel the boiled eggs, cut them into wedges and set aside.

Once the rice is cooked, return to a gentle heat and stir in the frozen
peas. Add the chillies/chiles and parsley, reserving some to garnish,
before finally adding the flaked mackerel and cream. Carefully stir all
of the ingredients together until evenly mixed and hot.

Transfer the kedgeree to serving dishes, decorate with the wedges of
egg and a sprinkling of parsley and serve at the table.

500 ml/2 cups fish stock/broth

400 g/14 oz. white fish fillets, skinned, chopped into 3-cm/1¼-inch cubes

400 g/14 oz. salmon fillets, skinned, chopped into 3-cm/1¼-inch cubes

1.5 kg/3 lb 5 oz. floury potatoes, peeled and chopped into chunks

100 ml/scant ½ cup double/heavy cream

1 teaspoon saffron strands, finely ground

50 g/3 tablespoons butter

1 tablespoon olive oil

1 leek, finely chopped

1 fennel bulb, finely chopped

50 ml/3½ tablespoons dry white wine

40 g/heaped ¼ cup plain/all-purpose flour

2 tablespoons finely chopped fresh parsley

grated zest of ½ lemon

squeeze of lemon juice

100 g/3½ oz. cooked peeled prawns/shrimp

salt and freshly ground black pepper

serves 4

Adding saffron to the mashed potato topping gives both colour and flavour. As they can be prepared in advance and then baked in the oven, these pretty fish pies are perfect for dinner party entertaining.

saffron fish pies

Bring the fish stock to the boil in a large saucepan. Add the fish cubes and simmer for 2–3 minutes until just cooked through. Remove with a slotted spoon and set aside to cool, reserving the stock.

Cook the potatoes in a large pan of boiling, salted water until tender; drain. While the potatoes are cooking, heat the double/heavy cream and saffron in a small pan, bring to the boil, then remove from the heat. Add 25 g/1½ tablespoons of the butter and the hot saffron cream to the potatoes and mash together well. Season with salt and freshly ground black pepper. Set aside.

Heat the olive oil in a frying pan/skillet. Gently fry the leek and fennel for 3 minutes until softened. Add the white wine and cook for 2–3 minutes until the wine is reduced and syrupy. Season with salt and freshly ground black pepper. Set aside.

Heat the remaining butter in a heavy-based saucepan until melted. Stir in the flour and cook, stirring, for 2 minutes. Gradually mix in the reserved fish stock. Cook, stirring, until the mixture comes to the boil and thickens to form a sauce. Season with salt and freshly ground black pepper. Stir in the parsley and lemon zest and juice.

Preheat the oven to 200°C (400°F) Gas 6.

Gently fold together the poached fish, prawns/shrimp, fried leek mixture and sauce. Divide between four small pie dishes, spreading it across the base. Top each one with an even layer of the saffron mash. Bake the pies in the preheated oven for 25–30 minutes until piping hot and lightly browned.

Alternatively, to make one large pie, bake in one large dish for 40 minutes until piping hot and lightly browned. Serve at once.

a handful of chopped fresh dill, stems discarded

400 g/14 oz. salmon, diced into bite-sized pieces

2 pinches of sea salt

250 g/9 oz. ready-made puff pastry

1 egg, lightly beaten

1 teaspoon English/hot mustard

a handful of fresh spinach leaves

6.5-cm/2½-inch round cookie cutter

serves 4

A Pithivier is a thing of delight! Traditionally a puff pastry parcel filled with almond paste and served as a dessert, they are now commonly made as a savoury dish. Think a delicious pie with buttery puff pastry and the wonderful combination of salmon and dill. If you purchase sides of salmon, save the offcuts in a bag in the freezer and make this dish when you have enough.

salmon and dill pithivier

Preheat the oven to 180°C (350°F) Gas 4.

Mix the dill and salmon together with a couple of pinches of sea salt in a large mixing bowl. Set aside.

Roll out the pastry on a lightly floured work surface to about a 4-mm/⅛-inch thickness. Cut 8 circles from the pastry using the round cookie cutter.

Cut four squares of baking parchment slightly bigger than the pastry circles and place four of the circles on them. Glaze the outer edges of these circles with the beaten egg to a width of about 2.5 cm/1 inch from the edge. Put ¼ teaspoon of mustard in the unglazed area in the middle of each and spread, before placing several spinach leaves on top to form a base. Place one-quarter of the salmon and dill mixture on top to form a mound. Gently stretch the centre of the unused pastry discs then carefully cover the mounds, sealing the pastry at the glazed edges. Use a fork to squeeze the edges together and trim off any excess pastry using the cookie cutter. Brush the pastry with the beaten egg and once the glaze has dried use a sharp knife to carefully score a spiral pattern on the tops of each pithivier.

Transfer each pithivier on its square of baking parchment to a baking sheet and bake in the preheated oven for 15 minutes until the pastry is golden brown. Serve immediately.

500 g/1 lb. purged clams

500 g/1 lb. mussels, cleaned and debearded

200 ml/¾ cup white wine

500 ml/2 cups fish stock/broth

25 g/1¾ tablespoons butter

100 g/3½ oz. smoked bacon, diced into 1-cm/½-inch lardons

2 teaspoons plain/ all-purpose flour, plus extra if needed

a pinch of saffron threads

500 g/1 lb. cod fillets, skinned, boned and diced

500 g/1 lb. ready-made puff pastry

1 egg, lightly beaten, to glaze

salt

serves 4–6

This is the type of feel-good, warming food you want to eat on a cold, dark evening with a group of friends and a few bottles of beer.

pastry-topped fish pie with bacon

Put the clams and mussels in a large saucepan with the wine. Set over a medium heat and cook until they just open. Remove the clams and mussels and shell them, discarding the shells. Set the fish aside.

Spoon the remaining liquor from the saucepan into the fish stock and stir. Be careful to leave any grit in the bottom of the pan behind.

Put the butter and bacon in a large saucepan set over a medium heat and cook until they are starting to caramelize. Spoon the lardons onto a plate and set aside, leaving the fat in the pan. Reduce the heat, add the flour to the pan and stir – it should be enough to form a crumbly mixture but add a little more flour if needed.

With the pan on the heat, slowly add the stock mixture, whisking until a thick paste is formed. Continue whisking until the mixture is the consistency of double/heavy cream. Add the saffron and whisk into the sauce. Season with a little salt.

Add the reserved clams, mussels and bacon with the cod to the sauce and mix together. Pour into a large casserole dish and set in the fridge to cool for at least 2 hours.

Preheat the oven to 160°C (325°F) Gas 3.

Roll out the pastry on a lightly floured work surface to a thickness of 4 mm/⅛ inch. Lift the pastry using the rolling pin and carefully drape over the casserole dish. Squeeze off the excess around the sides with your thumb and make gentle indentations with a fork around the edges. Brush the top with beaten egg. Using the leftover pastry, make fish shapes to decorate the top.

Bake in the preheated oven for 35 minutes, plus 5–10 minutes if using a deep casserole dish until the pastry is golden.

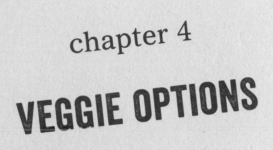

chapter 4

VEGGIE OPTIONS

200 g/2 cups macaroni or short penne pasta

40 g/3 tablespoons butter

1 bay leaf

40 g/5 tablespoons plain/all-purpose flour

600 ml/2½ cups full-fat/whole milk

125 g/1¼ cups Cheddar cheese, grated

1 teaspoon wholegrain mustard

grated fresh nutmeg

1 tablespoon sunflower oil

1 leek, finely chopped

200 g/6½ oz. button mushrooms, halved

100 g/3½ oz. vegetarian bacon, chopped (optional)

2 tablespoons grated Parmesan or other vegetarian hard cheese

25 g/⅓ cup fresh breadcrumbs

1 tablespoon pine nuts

salt and freshly ground black pepper

serves 4

Served warm from the oven, a hearty dish of macaroni cheese is a perennial favourite. Here, the rich cheese sauce is flavoured with bay and mustard, and combined with a tasty mixture of fried leeks and mushrooms. A crunchy topping gives the perfect finishing touch.

mushroom mac 'n' cheese

Preheat the oven to 200°C (400°F) Gas 6.

Cook the pasta in a large pan of boiling salted water following the package instructions, but until slightly underdone; drain.

Melt the butter with the bay leaf in a heavy-based saucepan. Mix in the flour and cook briefly, stirring. Gradually stir in the milk, mixing well with each addition. Cook, stirring, over a medium heat until the mixture thickens. Stir in the Cheddar cheese until melted. Stir in the mustard and season with nutmeg, salt and black pepper. Turn off the heat and set aside until needed.

Heat the oil in a frying pan/skillet over a low heat. Add the leek and fry gently for 5 minutes until softened, without allowing it to brown. Add the mushrooms, increase the heat, and fry briefly, stirring, until the mushrooms are lightly browned. Season with salt and freshly ground black pepper.

In a large bowl, mix together the cooked macaroni pasta, the mushroom mixture and the vegetarian bacon (if using). Mix in the cheese sauce. Tip into a shallow baking dish. Sprinkle with the Parmesan or other hard cheese, breadcrumbs and pine nuts. Bake in the preheated oven for 30 minutes until golden brown on top. Serve at once.

3 tablespoons olive oil

½ teaspoon chilli/hot red pepper flakes

100 g/3½ oz. Tenderstem cauliflower

300 g/10½ oz. jarred tomato sauce

150 g/5½ oz. fresh lasagne sheets

100 g/3½ oz. baby spinach

100 g/3½ oz. mixed-colour cherry tomatoes, halved

50 g/¾ cup finely grated Parmesan or other vegetarian hard cheese

mushroom sauce

20 g/1 cup dried porcini mushrooms

2 tablespoons olive oil

4 garlic cloves, crushed

250 g/9 oz. mixed mushrooms, sliced

1 sprig of fresh rosemary, leaves only

1 sprig of fresh thyme, leaves only

500 ml/2 cups crème fraîche or double/heavy cream

50 g/¾ cup finely grated Parmesan or other vegetarian hard cheese

salt and freshly ground black pepper

4 individual lasagne dishes (16 x 10 cm/6¼ x 4 inches)

serves 4

Nothing beats a lasagne, and using fresh pasta gives a more tender finish. With layers of tasty vegetables and rich creamy mushroom sauce, it is a serious treat for meat eaters and veggies alike.

individual cauli lasagnes

For the mushroom sauce, cover the dried porcini with boiling water and leave to rehydrate.

Heat the olive oil in a pan, add the garlic and cook for 1 minute, then add the mixed mushrooms, herbs and a pinch of salt and pepper. Cook until just starting to colour, stirring regularly. Add the porcini and soaking liquor. Leave to bubble and cook away, then reduce the heat, stir in the crème fraiche or cream and cook gently for a few minutes. Remove from the heat, stir in the Parmesan or other hard cheese and set aside.

Preheat the oven to 160°C (325°F) Gas 3.

In a frying pan/skillet, heat the olive oil and the chilli/hot red pepper flakes. Season the Tenderstem cauliflower and add to the pan – there is no need to cook it through, just fry until it has browned nicely on each side. Set aside.

To assemble, place a few spoonfuls of the jarred tomato sauce into each lasagne dish. Top with a fresh lasagne sheet (cut to size), some mushroom sauce, some spinach, another lasagne sheet, the halved cherry tomatoes and another lasagne sheet, and finish with the remaining tomato sauce and the final amount of mushroom sauce. Top each one with grated Parmesan or other hard cheese and the Tenderstem cauliflower.

Bake in the preheated oven for 40 minutes until the lasagnes are lightly browned on top and the sauce is bubbling.

500 g/1 lb. aubergines/eggplants

about 6 tablespoons olive oil

1 onion, finely chopped

1 leek, chopped

3 garlic cloves, chopped

1 carrot, peeled and
finely diced

6 tomatoes (about 750 g/
1⅔ lbs.), peeled and chopped

4 tablespoons tomato
purée/paste

½ teaspoon ground cinnamon

1 tablespoon dried oregano

2 fresh or dried bay leaves

1 teaspoon caster/
granulated sugar

200 g/1 cup dried Puy/French
green lentils

200 g/2 cups Pecorino or other
vegetarian hard cheese, grated

salt and freshly ground
black pepper

topping

3 eggs, beaten

30 g/¼ cup plain/
all-purpose flour

500 ml/16 fl oz. Greek yogurt

1 teaspoon salt

grated fresh nutmeg

serves 6

Popular throughout the Balkans, moussaka came to Britain in the fifties, and was received with such enthusiasm that it became almost a part of the national cuisine. This vegetarian version is food for the soul.

lentil moussaka

Preheat the oven to 180°C (350°F) Gas 4.

Cut the aubergines/eggplants into 1-cm/½-inch slices and brush the cut sides with olive oil. Heat a baking sheet with sides in the oven for 5 minutes, then bake the aubergine/eggplant slices, sprinkled with a little salt, for about 30 minutes, until beginning to brown. Halfway through cooking, turn them over with a spatula, so they cook evenly.

Meanwhile, heat 3 tablespoons of the olive oil in a frying pan/skillet and fry the onion, leek and garlic over a gentle heat until soft and golden. Add the diced carrot, chopped tomatoes, tomato pure/paste, cinnamon, oregano and bay leaves. Cover and simmer together for another 30 minutes or so. Stir in the sugar.

While the tomato sauce is cooking, rinse and drain the lentils, then place in a saucepan covered with cold water. Bring to the boil and simmer for about 20 minutes, until soft (bear in mind that they will not cook any further once mixed with the tomato sauce.) Drain the lentils and add to the tomato sauce, then season with salt and pepper.

Generously butter a deep ovenproof dish and spread half of the aubergine/eggplant slices in the bottom. Cover with half of the tomato and lentil mixture, then repeat with another layer of each. Sprinkle half of the grated cheese over the surface.

To make the topping, whisk the eggs with the flour, then gently stir in the yogurt, salt and some pepper and a little grated nutmeg.

Spoon the mixture over the dish of vegetables, finishing by sprinkling the remaining grated cheese over the surface. Bake in the preheated oven for 30–40 minutes, until the top is bubbling and brown.

1 tablespoon olive oil

1 onion, chopped

1 garlic clove, chopped

1 celery stalk, chopped

½ red (bell) pepper, deseeded and finely chopped

150 g/5 oz. field mushrooms, finely chopped

1 teaspoon ground cumin

pinch of dried oregano

½ teaspoon smoked paprika

1 x 400-g/14-oz. can of chopped tomatoes

1 teaspoon chipotle paste

pinch of sugar

1 x 400-g/14-oz. can of kidney beans in water, drained and rinsed

200 g/6½ oz. button mushrooms, halved if large

salt and freshly ground black pepper

chopped fresh coriander/ cilantro, to garnish

sour cream, to serve

grated Cheddar cheese, to serve

serves 4

This spicy vegetarian take on a classic chilli con carne is both simple and quick to make. It can also, usefully, be made a day in advance and kept in the fridge until needed. Serve with freshly baked cornbread, warm from the oven, or baked potatoes. It's especially good with tangy sour cream, which contrasts nicely with this rich tomato-based dish.

mushroom and bean chilli

Heat the oil over a medium heat in a casserole dish. Add the onion, garlic, celery and red (bell) pepper and fry, stirring, for 5 minutes until softened. Add the field mushrooms, cumin, oregano and smoked paprika and fry, stirring, for 5 minutes.

Add the chopped tomatoes, 200 ml/1 scant cup of water, chipotle paste and sugar. Season with salt and pepper and stir well. Bring to the boil, then stir in the kidney beans and button mushrooms.

Reduce the heat to medium and simmer, uncovered, for 15 minutes, stirring now and then.

Portion into bowls and garnish with the chopped coriander/cilantro. Serve with sour cream and grated Cheddar cheese, if desired.

1 tablespoon olive oil

1 onion, chopped

1 garlic clove, chopped

1 celery stalk, thinly sliced

1 red (bell) pepper, deseeded and finely chopped

200 g/3 cups mushrooms, thickly sliced

1 tablespoon tomato purée/paste

1 x 400-g/14-oz. can chopped tomatoes

a pinch of dried oregano

1 x 400-g/14-oz. can borlotti beans, drained and rinsed

1 x 400-g/14-oz. can butter/ lima beans, drained and rinsed

2 tablespoons chopped fresh parsley

900 g/2 lb. potatoes, peeled and chopped into chunks

25 g/1½ tablespoons butter

splash of full-fat/whole milk

2 teaspoons wholegrain mustard

25 g/¼ cup grated Cheddar cheese

salt and freshly ground black pepper

serves 4–6

This different take on a meat-based Shepherd's Pie is ideal for a simple, hearty midweek meal. Serve it with green beans, broccoli or peas on the side.

gardener's pie

Preheat the oven to 200°C (400°F) Gas 6.

Heat the olive oil in a large frying pan/skillet. Fry the onion gently for 3 minutes, stirring now and then, until softened. Add the garlic, celery and red (bell) pepper and fry until just softened. Add the mushrooms and fry, stirring, until they are lightly coloured.

Mix in the tomato purée/paste, then the chopped tomatoes. Season with the oregano and salt and freshly ground black pepper. Bring to the boil, then reduce the heat and simmer for 5 minutes. Add the borlotti and butter/lima beans and the parsley. Cook for a further 5 minutes.

Meanwhile, cook the potatoes in a large pan of boiling, salted water until tender; drain. Mash the potatoes with the butter and milk, seasoning with black pepper. Mix in the mustard thoroughly.

Place the bean mixture in an ovenproof dish. Top with the mustard mash, spreading it in an even layer. Use a fork to texture the mash and then sprinkle with the Cheddar cheese.

Bake in the preheated oven for 30 minutes until heated through and the cheese has melted. Serve at once.

150 g/1 cup plus 3 tablespoons spelt flour, plus extra for dusting

75 g/5 tablespoons butter, cubed

2 tablespoons cold water

filling

1 tablespoon olive oil

1 shallot, chopped

300 g/10 oz. white/cup mushrooms, sliced 1-cm/½-inch thick

300 g/1¼ cups double/heavy cream

2 whole eggs

1 egg yolk

grated fresh nutmeg

100 g/3½ oz. blue cheese, crumbled into small chunks

50 g/⅓ cup walnut pieces

salt and freshly ground black pepper

24-cm/9½-inch loose-based fluted tart pan, lightly greased

baking beans

makes 1 quiche

Mushroom quiche is a much-loved classic. In this version, a nutty tasting spelt flour crust encases a rich filling made from fried mushrooms and shallots, combined with savoury blue cheese. Serve with a refreshing watercress or radicchio salad for contrast.

mushroom, blue cheese and walnut quiche

For the pastry, place the flour, a pinch of salt and the butter in a food processor. Pulse until the butter has been absorbed by the flour. Add the cold water and blend until the mixture forms a dough. Wrap the pastry in clingfilm/plastic wrap and chill in the fridge for 30 minutes.

For the filling, heat the olive oil in a frying pan/skillet. Fry the shallot over a medium heat for 2 minutes, until softened. Add the mushrooms and fry over a high heat, until lightly browned. Drain any liquid in a colander and allow to cool.

Preheat the oven to 200°C (400°F) Gas 6.

Roll out the pastry on a lightly floured work surface. Line the greased pan with the pastry, pressing it in firmly. Prick the base several times with a fork. Line the case with baking parchment and fill with baking beans. Blind bake the pastry case in the preheated oven for 15 minutes. Carefully remove the parchment and beans and bake for a further 5 minutes, then remove from the oven. Leave the oven on.

Meanwhile, whisk together the cream, eggs and egg yolk. Season with salt, black pepper and grated nutmeg. Sprinkle the blue cheese and walnuts in an even layer inside the pastry case. Top with the fried mushrooms and pour over the cream mixture. Bake for 40 minutes. Leave to cool slightly, and serve warm or at room temperature.

2 large baking potatoes

100 g/generous 1 cup
Cheddar cheese, grated

1 egg, beaten

1 heaped teaspoon
wholegrain mustard

2 teaspoons Worcestershire
sauce, plus extra to serve

1 heaped tablespoon butter

salt and freshly ground
black pepper

green salad, to serve

serves 2

This humble dish, originating from Wales, is hard to beat for comfort-factor. Welsh rarebit has its origins as long ago as the 15th century and used to be called 'Caws Pobi' – literally baked cheese. It is really just posh cheese on toast – but wow, it is good! This is a pleasingly filling potato version.

Welsh rarebit baked potatoes

Preheat the oven to 200°C (400°F) Gas 6.

Prick the skin of your potatoes and rub with a little salt. Place in the preheated oven for about 1 hour, depending on the size of your potatoes. To test if they are cooked, insert a sharp knife and if the potato feels soft inside with no resistance to the knife, it is done. If you still feel some resistance, cook for a little while longer.

When the potatoes have almost finished cooking in the oven, prepare the rarebit topping. Mix the grated cheese into the egg with the mustard and Worcestershire sauce. Season with salt and pepper.

Preheat the grill/broiler to high.

When cool enough to handle, cut each potato in half. Scoop out the soft potato flesh into a bowl, leaving the skins with enough potato on so that they hold their shape and mash with the butter, then season with salt and pepper. Spoon the mashed potato back into the potato skins and place on a baking sheet.

Spoon a quarter of the rarebit mixture over each potato half and grill/broil for about 5 minutes, until the mixture has puffed up and the cheese has started to turn golden brown on top. Remove from the grill/broiler and serve straight away with a green salad. Top with a dash of extra Worcestershire sauce just before serving.

pastry

225 g/1¾ cups plain/all-purpose flour, plus extra for dusting

pinch of salt

125 g/½ cup plus 1 tablespoon butter, cubed

2–3 tablespoons cold water

filling

400 g/14 oz. potatoes, peeled and cut into chunks

2 onions, quartered and thinly sliced

1 tablespoon vegetable or sunflower oil

25 g/1½ tablespoons butter

grated fresh nutmeg

100 g/1 cup plus 2 tablespoons grated Cheddar cheese

2 tablespoons chopped fresh parsley

full-fat/whole milk, for brushing

salt and freshly ground black pepper

20-cm/8-inch deep, loose-based fluted tart pan, greased

serves 4–6

A homely recipe, which everyone will enjoy. The crisp, buttery pastry contrasts nicely with the soft, cheesy potato filling. Serve with green vegetables to cut through the richness of the cheese.

potato cheese pie

First, make the pastry. Mix together the flour and salt, then rub in the butter with your fingertips until absorbed. Mix in the cold water until the mixture comes together to form a dough. Wrap in clingfilm/plastic wrap and chill in the fridge for 30 minutes.

For the filling, cook the potatoes in a large pan of boiling, salted water until tender; drain.

Meanwhile, gently fry the onions in the oil over a low heat, stirring often, for 10 minutes, until thoroughly softened.

Mash the cooked potatoes thoroughly with the butter. Season well with freshly grated nutmeg, salt and freshly ground black pepper. Stir in the Cheddar cheese, fried onions and parsley. Set aside to cool.

Preheat the oven to 200°C (400°F) Gas 6.

Roll out two-thirds of the pastry on a lightly floured work surface. Use the pastry to line the greased tart pan, pressing it in well. Fill the pastry case with the potato mixture.

Roll out the remaining pastry and cut out a pie lid. Brush the edges of the pie case with milk and top with the pie lid, pressing the edges together to seal. Brush the pastry lid with milk and cut three slashes in the centre of the pie.

Bake the pie in the preheated oven for 50 minutes until golden brown. Serve hot, warm or at room temperature.

2 tablespoons olive oil

1 large red onion, halved and thinly sliced

2 sprigs of fresh thyme, leaves only

¼ teaspoon white sugar

1 teaspoon balsamic vinegar

2 teaspoons butter

2 large, flat mushrooms, stalks removed

salt and freshly ground black pepper

to serve

burger buns, halved

mayonnaise

iceberg lettuce

thin slices of Camembert cheese

Triple-cooked Fries (see page 108)

serves 2

Creamy Camembert cheese pairs well with mushrooms in this flavourful, vegetarian take on the classic hamburger. Simple to make and utterly delicious – pub grub at its best.

mushroom burgers

Heat 1 tablespoon of the olive oil in a large, heavy frying pan/skillet. Add the red onion and thyme and fry gently over a low heat for 8 minutes, stirring now and then, until softened. Add the sugar and vinegar and fry for 2 minutes more until caramelized. Set aside.

Wipe the frying pan/skillet clean. Heat the remaining 1 tablespoon olive oil and butter over a medium heat. Add the mushrooms and fry for 5 minutes, turning often, until browned on both sides. Season with salt and freshly ground black pepper.

Preheat the grill/broiler to medium.

Briefly grill/broil the burger buns, cut-side up, until just golden.

To assemble the burgers, spread the bottom half buns with mayonnaise. Layer lettuce, a mushroom, Camembert cheese and half the caramelized onions in each bun. Top with the toasted bun lids and serve at once with triple cooked fries.

chapter 5

SIDES AND SAUCES

This recipe produces golden brown chips/fries, which are crisp on the outside and tender inside – a truly tempting combination. They make the perfect side for pretty much every savoury dish in this book – and if you end up with double carbs, it's not a problem.

triple-cooked fries

800 g/1 lb 7 oz. chipping potatoes, such as Maris Piper or Idaho, peeled

vegetable or sunflower oil, for deep-frying

salt

serves 4

Cut the potatoes into 1-cm/½-inch-thick fingers. Rinse the chips/fries 2–3 times in cold water to wash out excess starch.

Place the potatoes in a large pan and cover with cold, salted water. Bring to the boil, then reduce the heat and simmer for 5 minutes; drain. Cover the par-boiled chips/fries with cold water to cool them, drain and chill in the fridge for 30 minutes to firm them up.

Preheat the oil in a deep fat fryer or large heavy-based saucepan to 130°C (250°F).

Add the chilled chips/fries, cooking in batches so as not to overcrowd the pan, and fry each batch for 5 minutes. They should remain pale and not take on any colour. Remove with a slotted spoon, drain on kitchen paper and allow to cool.

Heat the same oil for deep-frying in the deep fat fryer or large heavy-based pan to a temperature of 180°C (350°F). Add the cooled chips/fries, frying them in batches so as not to overcrowd the pan, until golden brown and crisp, around 3–5 minutes. Remove with a slotted spoon, drain on kitchen paper, season with salt and serve at once.

1 kg/2 lb 4 oz. waxy potatoes

2 tablespoons olive oil

salt

1 garlic bulb, broken up into
individual garlic cloves

8 sprigs of rosemary, cut into
2.5-cm/1-inch pieces

serves 6

Very simple indeed to make, these roast potatoes with their beautiful Mediterranean flavours are a pleasure to eat! Serve them as a summery side dish with grilled meats or fish.

rosemary garlic potatoes

Preheat the oven to 220°C (425°F) Gas 7.

Peel the potatoes and, depending on their size, cut them into quarters or halves; you want them to be evenly sized to ensure even cooking.

Bring a large pan of salted water to the boil. Add the potatoes and boil for 10 minutes until par-boiled. Drain them thoroughly, return to the pan and shake them in the pan to roughen their surfaces.

Add the olive oil to a roasting pan, place in the oven and heat through until the oil becomes very hot.

Add the potato chunks to the hot olive oil, tossing and turning them to coat them evenly in it, then season with salt. Add the garlic cloves and rosemary, mixing well. Roast in the preheated oven for around 40–45 minutes until the potatoes are golden brown all over, turning now and then to ensure even browning. Serve at once.

800 g/1 lb 7 oz. floury potatoes, peeled and chopped

100 g/7 tablespoons cold butter, cubed

1 teaspoon truffle oil

salt and freshly ground black pepper

serves 4

This smooth-textured mashed potato with its subtle truffle flavour is a rich treat. Serve it with grilled/broiled steak or roast beef or roast chicken for a decadent meal.

truffle mash

Cook the potatoes in a large saucepan of boiling, salted water until tender; drain.

Place a potato ricer over a pan and pass the freshly drained potatoes through it. Alternatively, mash the potatoes using a potato masher.

Add the butter, a few cubes at a time, and, using a fork, fold into the potato. Season with salt and freshly ground black pepper. Add the truffle oil and fold in well. Serve at once.

3–4 floury potatoes, peeled and quartered

20 g/1½ tablespoons butter

40 g/½ cup finely grated Parmesan cheese (optional)

2 tablespoons double/heavy cream

salt and freshly ground black pepper

serves 4

Potatoes, butter, cheese and cream – what's not to love about this luxurious mash? It's the perfect partner for pie, lamb shanks or toad in the hole.

creamy mashed potatoes

Cook the potatoes in a large saucepan of boiling, salted water until tender; drain.

Return the potatoes to the pan. Add the butter and mash until lovely and soft. Mix in the Parmesan, if using, and then the double/heavy cream, salt and pepper. Serve immediately with extra black pepper.

500 g/1 lb. even-sized waxy potatoes

2 tablespoons extra virgin olive oil

grated zest of ½ lemon

1 teaspoon freshly squeezed lemon juice

2 tablespoons chopped fresh chives

2 tablespoons chopped fresh mint leaves

3 tablespoons finely chopped fresh parsley

salt and freshly ground black pepper

serves 4

Crushing potatoes is a very easy way of preparing them, as no peeling is required! The roughly crushed potatoes soak up the flavours of the dressing, while the use of lemon zest and herbs give a real lift to the dish. Try them with Salmon Fishcakes (see page 72) or Chicken Kievs (see page 37).

herby crushed potatoes

Cook the potatoes in a large pan of boiling, salted water until tender; drain and return to the pan. Use a fork to roughly crush them.

Add the olive oil, lemon zest and juice and season with salt and freshly ground black pepper, mixing well. Add the chives, mint and parsley and mix in. Serve warm or at room temperature.

8–10 new potatoes

20 g/1½ tablespoons butter

salt and freshly ground black pepper

serves 2

These simple little well-seasoned and buttered new potatoes make a lovely accompaniment to plenty of main meals in this book.

buttery crushed potatoes

Preheat the grill/broiler to medium.

Cook the new potatoes (skins on) in a large pan of boiling, salted water until tender; drain and return to the pan.

Add the butter and swirl to melt. Tip the buttery potatoes onto a greased baking sheet and crush with a fork. Sprinkle salt and pepper on the top and pop under the preheated grill/broiler for 5 minutes to brown.

1 kg/2 lb 4 oz. potatoes, peeled

2 tablespoons goose fat

salt

serves 6

Cooking potatoes in goose fat is a simple but effective way of ensuring gloriously crispy on the outside, fluffy on the inside roasties! Serve these with Best-ever Roast Chicken (see page 65) or a roasted centrepiece of your choice for a Sunday family meal or dinner with hungry friends.

goose fat roast potatoes

Preheat the oven to 220°C (425°F) Gas 7.

Depending on their size, cut the potatoes into quarters or halves; you want them to be evenly sized in order to ensure even cooking.

Cook the potatoes in a large pan of salted, boiling water for 10 minutes until par-boiled. Drain them thoroughly, return to the pan and shake them in the pan to roughen their surfaces.

Add the goose fat to a roasting pan, place in the preheated oven and heat through so that the fat melts and becomes very hot.

Add the potato chunks to the hot goose fat, tossing and turning them to coat them evenly in it. Season with salt and then roast in the preheated oven for around 40–45 minutes until golden brown on all sides, turning now and then to ensure even browning. Serve at once.

150 g/1½ cups spinach

50 g/2 oz. canned anchovies, drained

4 garlic cloves, peeled

6 floury potatoes, peeled

3 brown onions, peeled

300 ml/1¼ cups double/ heavy cream

20 x 25-cm/8 x 10-inch casserole dish, greased

serves 4

This recipe uses the saltiness of canned anchovies in an unusual way to deliver a satisfying side dish. Serve as an accompaniment to roasted meats, stews or pies.

potato, spinach and anchovy bake

Preheat the oven to 160°C (325°F) Gas 3.

Put the spinach and 50 ml/3½ tablespoons of water in a saucepan set over a medium heat. Cover and cook until steam forms, then immediately remove from the heat. The spinach will wilt.

Transfer the wilted spinach and its cooking liquor to a food processor. Add the anchovies and garlic and blend to a purée. Pour into a bowl and set aside.

Using a slicing blade, very thinly slice the potatoes in the food processor – do not rinse the potatoes after this as the starch binds the dish together. Very thinly slice the onions in the same way.

Arrange a thin layer of potatoes on the base of the casserole dish. Using a pastry brush or with a spoon, thinly coat the potato layer with the anchovy, garlic and spinach purée. Next, add a very thin layer of onions. Repeat this layering process as many times as possible, finishing with a layer of potato. Ensure there is enough room left at the top of the dish for expansion while cooking (about 1 cm/½-inch).

Pour over most of the cream and leave it to settle for 10 minutes, before adding more cream until the top is just covered.

Cover with foil and bake in the preheated oven for 1½ hours. Check after 1 hour, then at 15 minute intervals – when the potato is soft increase the oven temperature to 180°C (350°F) Gas 4 and remove the foil for 10 minutes to brown the top. Slice and serve.

Tip If you do not have a slicing blade for the food processor, you could slice the potatoes and onion using a mandoline or with care using a small sharp knife by hand.

Yorkshire batter

250 g/1¾ cups plus 2 tablespoons plain/all-purpose flour

150 ml/⅔ cup full-fat/whole milk

4 eggs, beaten

2 tablespoons sunflower oil

salt

12-hole muffin pan, large roasting pan or ovenproof frying pan/skillet, greased

baby leek variation

150 g/5½ oz. baby leeks, halved widthways and trimmed

5 sprigs of fresh thyme

1 tablespoon olive oil

1 x quantity Yorkshire Batter

12-hole muffin pan, greased

grape variation

150 g/5½ oz. red seedless grapes

1 tablespoon runny honey

1 x quantity Yorkshire batter

salt and freshly ground black pepper

ovenproof frying pan/ skillet, greased

makes 12 individual or 1 large

This Yorkshire pudding recipe works perfectly well on its own, but if you feel you want to add an extra element, the grape or leek variations are delicious.

Yorkshire puddings two ways

Sift the flour into a large bowl with a large pinch of salt. Combine the milk in a jug/pitcher with 150 ml/⅔ cup water. Make a well in the middle of the flour and add the eggs. Pour in a little milk and water, then whisk together into a smooth batter. Mix in the rest of the liquid, until you have a batter the consistency of single/light cream. Leave to stand at room temperature for at least 15 minutes.

Preheat the oven to 230°C (450°F) Gas 8 and put your chosen greased pan on a high shelf for 10 minutes to preheat. If using a roasting pan or frying pan/skillet, take out of the oven and place on the hob/stovetop over a medium heat while you pour in the batter. If using a muffin pan, simply quickly pour in the batter and return to the oven. If it doesn't immediately sizzle when added, preheat the pan a little more. Cook the Yorkshires in the preheated oven for 15–20 minutes until well risen and golden. Watch towards the end of the cooking time, but don't open the door early or your puddings will sink.

baby leek variation

Sauté the baby leeks with the thyme in the olive oil in a frying pan/skillet over a medium heat for 6 minutes. Preheat the muffin pan as instructed (above). Ladle in the batter, then quickly top each with the sautéed leeks and cook in the preheated oven as instructed above.

grape variation

Preheat the oven to 200°C (400°F) Gas 6 and put the pan/skillet in to warm for 10 minutes. Put the grapes into the hot pan/skillet, then drizzle with the honey and season with salt and pepper. Roast in the preheated oven for 8 minutes. Quickly pour in the batter and cook in the preheated oven at 230°C (450°F) Gas 8 as instructed above.

½ cauliflower, cut into florets

2 courgettes/zucchini, thinly sliced on an angle

100 g/3½ oz. Brussels sprouts, thinly sliced

70 g/5 tablespoons butter

40 g/5 tablespoons plain/all-purpose flour

1 litre/quart full-fat/whole milk

200 g/scant 2 cups grated Gruyère cheese

1 teaspoon chopped fresh thyme

½ teaspoon grated fresh nutmeg

50 g/⅔ cup dried breadcrumbs

salt and freshly ground black pepper

serves 6

A delicious alternative to a carb-filled potato gratin, yet still sublimely indulgent and comforting.

cheesy vegetable gratin

Preheat the oven to 190°C (375°F) Gas 5.

Steam the cauliflower in a large pan of boiling water fitted with a steamer basket for 5–7 minutes, until the florets are just tender. Rinse them in cold water, drain, and arrange them in a single layer in the buttered dish. Add the raw sliced courgettes/zucchini and sprouts.

In a large saucepan over a medium heat, melt the butter and whisk in the flour until it forms a smooth paste. Continue whisking and cook for about 2 minutes, then gradually add the milk, a little at a time. Add half the cheese and stir until melted. Continue whisking and cook until the sauce is heated through, smooth and thickened. Remove from the heat and season with salt, the thyme and nutmeg.

Pour 500 ml/2 cups of the béchamel sauce over the cauliflower, courgettes/zucchini and sprouts, and gently toss the florets to make sure they are thoroughly coated with the sauce. Bake the gratin, uncovered, in the preheated oven for 15 minutes.

Stir together the remaining grated Gruyère cheese and the breadcrumbs and sprinkle them over the gratin. Bake for an additional 10–15 minutes, until the gratin is hot and bubbly and the cheese is melted and browned. Sprinkle the surface of the baked gratin with black pepper and serve hot.

red wine gravy

2 tablespoons olive oil

20 g/1½ tablespoons butter

2 red onions, thinly sliced

2 garlic cloves, crushed

1 sprig of fresh rosemary

1 tablespoon tomato
purée/paste

1 tablespoon plain/
all-purpose flour

175 ml/¾ cup red wine

175 ml/¾ cup beef stock/broth

salt and ground black pepper

porcini gravy

25 g/¾ oz. dried porcini

2 tablespoons olive oil

3 banana shallots, thinly sliced

20 g/1½ tablespoons butter

1 garlic clove, crushed

1 tablespoon plain/
all-purpose flour

75 ml/⅓ cup red wine

roasting meat juices

salt and ground black pepper

simple roast chicken gravy

roasting meat juices

2⅓ tablespoons plain/
all-purpose flour

350 ml/1½ cups hot chicken
stock/broth

salt and ground black pepper

each serves 4–6

Here we have three options to suit every gravy mood. Take your pick and enjoy with a roast dinner, toad in the hole or poured over a plate of chips/fries.

gravy three ways

red wine gravy

Heat a frying pan/skillet over a medium heat. Add the oil, heat for 1 minute, then add the butter. Once the butter has melted, tip in the onions, stir and cook until golden. Add the garlic and rosemary, stir and cook for 1 minute. Stir in the tomato purée/paste and cook for 1 minute. Add the flour and stir in. Pour in the red wine and beef stock/broth. Bring to the boil, season lightly with salt and a generous amount of black pepper, then reduce the heat and simmer for 15 minutes until thickened. Remove the rosemary sprig and serve.

porcini gravy

Soak the mushrooms for at least half an hour in hand-hot water. Drain, retaining the soaking liquid, and roughly chop the mushrooms.

Heat the oil in a shallow pan and add the sliced shallots. Cook over a low heat until beginning to soften. Stir in the butter, then add the crushed garlic. Cook for another 5 minutes or so until the shallots start to turn golden. Add the flour, stir and cook for a minute, then pour in the wine. Allow to reduce and thicken, then add the mushrooms and their soaking liquid. Bring to the boil, then reduce the heat and simmer for 15 minutes.

Add any meat juices or add the gravy to the juices in a meat roasting pan. Sieve/strain, then reheat if needed and serve.

simple roast chicken gravy

Put the meat juices in a pan over medium heat. Sprinkle the flour into the pan and stir into the pan juices until you get a paste. Gradually whisk in the hot stock/broth, then bring to the boil and simmer for about 5 minutes, adding a little extra stock/broth if it's too thick. Season with salt and pepper to taste. Serve.

tomato ketchup

1 kg/2 lb 4 oz. tomatoes

150 ml/generous ½ cup vinegar

50 g/¼ cup soft dark brown sugar

½ teaspoon fine salt

pinch of ground cinnamon

pinch of ground cloves

pinch of celery salt

curry ketchup

1 small onion, grated

2 tablespoons vegetable oil

2 tablespoons curry powder

1 tablespoon hot paprika

½ teaspoon mustard powder

pinch of ground cloves

500 g/1 lb. passata/strained tomatoes

6 tablespoons dark brown sugar

125 ml/½ cup malt vinegar

salt

chilli ketchup

1 small onion, finely chopped

1 tablespoon vegetable oil

1 garlic clove, crushed

700 g/1½ lb. passata/strained tomatoes

¼ teaspoon chilli/hot red pepper flakes

1 teaspoon tomato ketchup

splash of cider vinegar

salt and ground black pepper

Everyone loves the classic version of this condiment and it is a fail-safe, versatile option. The home-made version is even better, and the curry or chilli variations really take things up a notch. Perfect for dipping all manner of pub grub, whether chips/fries (of course), Scotch eggs, onion rings or goujons.

ketchup three ways

tomato ketchup

Roughly chop the tomatoes and remove the cores. Put the tomatoes in a saucepan and cook over medium-high heat, stirring occasionally, until they break down; 15–20 minutes. Transfer to a food processor and blend until smooth, then rub through a fine-mesh sieve/strainer and return the paste to a clean pan. Continue cooking the tomato pulp over a low heat, stirring often, until very thick. Stir in the remaining ingredients and simmer for 5 minutes. Taste and adjust seasoning, adding more vinegar and/or sugar according to taste. The sauce will keep, covered, in the fridge for at least 1 week.

curry ketchup

Put the onion and the oil in a saucepan and cook until softened over a medium heat. Stir in all the spices and cook until aromatic, about 1 minute more. Add the passata/strained tomatoes, sugar, vinegar and salt to taste. Stir to dissolve and bring to the boil, then lower the heat and simmer until thick. Taste and adjust seasoning. The sauce will keep, covered, in the fridge for at least 1 week.

chilli ketchup

Put the onion and the oil in a saucepan and cook until softened over a medium heat. Stir in the garlic, passata/strained tomatoes, chilli/hot red pepper flakes and ketchup and bring to the boil, then lower the heat and simmer until thick. Add some salt, pepper and a splash of vinegar; taste and adjust seasoning. It will keep, covered, in the fridge for at least 1 week.

chapter 6

DESSERTS

500 g/1 lb. ready-made
shortcrust pastry

plain/all-purpose flour,
for dusting

lemon filling

freshly squeezed juice
of 8 lemons and grated zest
of 3 lemons

250 g/1¼ cups caster/
granulated sugar

80 g/generous ¼ cup cornflour/
cornstarch

4 egg yolks (whites reserved for
the meringue below)

100 g/7 tablespoons butter

meringue

5 egg whites

6 tablespoons caster/
granulated sugar

*23-cm/9-inch loose-based,
fluted tart pan, greased*

baking beans

serves 8

With a tangy and vibrant lemon custard and a billowing
cloud of meringue topping, lemon meringue pie is a
proper feel-good dessert.

lemon meringue pie

Roll out the pastry on a lightly floured work surface to a thin circle just
larger than the size of your tart pan. Carefully move the pastry into the
prepared tart pan and press it down so that it fits snugly. Trim away
any excess pastry with a knife, but leave some pastry hanging over the
edge of the pan. This will be trimmed after the tart is baked. Prick the
base with a fork and chill in the fridge for 30 minutes.

Preheat the oven to 200°C (400°F) Gas 6.

Line the pastry with baking parchment, fill with baking beans and blind
bake in the preheated oven for about 20–25 minutes, until lightly
golden brown. Remove from the oven and remove the baking beans
and parchment. Trim the pastry using a sharp knife so that it is level
with the top of the pan. Leave to cool. Reduce the oven temperature
to 180°C (350°F) Gas 4.

For the filling, place the lemon juice, zest and sugar in a saucepan with
500 ml/generous 2 cups water and bring to the boil. Remove from the
heat and leave to cool. Whisk the cornflour/cornstarch with 120 ml/8
tablespoons of the cooled lemon syrup and beat in the egg yolks. Heat
the remaining lemon syrup again and whisk in the cornflour/cornstarch
mixture. Stir constantly over the heat, until the mixture thickens. Add
the butter to the pan and beat hard. Let cool, then pour into the pastry
case. If any lumps have formed in the lemon custard, pass the mixture
through a sieve/strainer, pressing it through with the back of a spoon.

For the meringue, whisk the egg whites to stiff peaks. Add the sugar, a
spoonful at a time, whisking constantly until the meringue is smooth
and glossy. Spoon the meringue over the top of the lemon custard and
swirl into peaks. Bake in the preheated oven for 25–30 minutes, until
the meringue is golden brown and set. Remove from the oven and let
cool completely before serving.

500 ml/2 cups full-fat/
whole milk

100 g/½ cup caster/
granulated sugar

1 teaspoon pure vanilla extract

3 eggs

7–10 slices of white bread,
cut about 5-mm/¼-inch thick

150 g/1¼ cups raisins

butter, softened, for spreading

50 g/¼ cup caster/granulated
sugar mixed with 1 tablespoon
ground cinnamon, for sprinkling

26 x 18-cm/10 x 7-inch or
30 x 20-cm/12 x 8-inch baking
dish, greased

serves 4

This recipe is so easy to make and with delicious results. It tastes even better with slightly older bread, so remember not to throw it away!

bread and butter pudding

First make the custard mixture. Add the milk to a small mixing bowl, then whisk in the sugar and vanilla extract using a balloon whisk until dissolved. Add the eggs and mix with the balloon whisk until you have a smooth mixture. Put the mixture to one side.

See how many slices of bread will fit in a criss-cross pattern in your baking dish, then spread each slice generously with butter.

Sprinkle three-quarters of the raisins on the bottom of the prepared baking dish. Place the buttered bread back in the dish, then sprinkle the remaining raisins on top. Whisk the custard mixture that you put to one side and pour it on top of the bread. The bread will float up to the top of the dish, but don't worry, this is perfectly normal. Leave to soak for 1 hour in the fridge so the custard mixture can be absorbed into the bread.

Preheat the oven to 100°C (210°F) Gas ¼.

Bake the pudding in the preheated oven for 50–70 minutes until the custard has set. The low temperature ensures that the custard won't separate and go lumpy. You can check to see if it's ready by carefully removing the pan from the oven and shaking from side to side. If the custard is set but wobbles slightly when you shake it, it's ready.

Sprinkle the top of the pudding with the sugar and cinnamon mix and allow to cool before serving.

sablé pastry

200 g/1½ cups plain/
all-purpose flour

100 g/7 tablespoons butter,
at room temperature

20 g/scant ¼ cup
ground almonds

60 g/7 tablespoons icing/
confectioners' sugar, plus extra
for dusting

1 egg yolk, plus 1 egg yolk,
lightly beaten, to glaze

filling

50 g/3½ tablespoons butter

50 ml/3½ tablespoons double/
heavy cream

1 egg

400 g/1¼ cups golden/
light corn syrup

100 g/scant 2 cups fresh
brown breadcrumbs

6 small fluted tart pans or rings

makes 8

Treacle tart is a British classic. It's the perfect comfort food on a cold day, served warm with cream. If you don't want to make the pastry, use a good quality store-bought one.

individual treacle tarts

For the sablé pastry, in a food processor, blend the flour, butter and ground almonds together before adding the icing/confectioners' sugar and then the egg yolk. Continue to blend until the mixture comes together into a dough. Roll the dough out to a thickness of about 2 cm/¾ inch. Wrap it in some clingfilm/plastic wrap and place in the fridge to chill for 1 hour.

Preheat the oven to 160°C (325°F) Gas 3.

Divide the chilled pastry into six and roll each of these portions out to a thickness of about 3 mm/⅛ inch – dusting the pastry with a little icing/confectioners' sugar will stop it sticking. Place the pastry into the small tart pans or rings and press it down so that it fits snugly. Place the tart bases in the fridge for a further 30 minutes.

Prick the tart bases with a fork to stop them rising and bake in the preheated oven for 10 minutes to 'set' the pastry; it should be just cooked but still pale. Brush the tart bases with the beaten egg yolk before returning them to the oven for a further 3 minutes to glaze them. Reduce the oven temperature to 140°C (280°F) Gas 1.

For the filling, heat the butter over a low heat in a heavy-based saucepan until it is foaming and just starting to turn brown. Take off the heat and immediately add the cream and whisk until cool. Add the egg, then the golden/light corn syrup and whisk to combine fully before adding the breadcrumbs. Mix well, then pour into the tart bases. Bake in the preheated oven for 30 minutes, then remove and cool for at least 15 minutes before serving. Serve fresh from the oven or, if they have cooled completely, reheated for 5 minutes in a low oven. Serve with cream and fresh raspberries.

500 g/1 lb. ready-made
shortcrust pastry

1 egg, lightly beaten

apple filling

4 cooking apples,
peeled and cored

4 dessert apples,
peeled and cored

freshly squeezed
juice of 1 lemon

2 teaspoons ground cinnamon

60 g/generous ¼ cup soft light
brown sugar

115 g/generous ½ cup caster/
granulated sugar, plus extra for
sprinkling

2 tablespoons plain/all-purpose
flour, plus extra for dusting

1 teaspoon pure vanilla extract

a pinch of salt

60 g/½ stick butter, cubed

*23-cm/9-inch round pie dish,
greased*

serves 6–8

Crisp, buttery pastry with deep layers of apple scented with cinnamon spices and vanilla – there are few more comforting desserts. This recipe uses a combination of dessert and cooking apples to balance the sharpness of the fruit, but you can use only cooking apples, if you prefer.

classic apple pie

Preheat the oven to 200°C (400°F) Gas 6.

Divide the pastry in half. Roll out one half of the pastry on a lightly floured work surface into a circle just larger than the size of your pie dish. Carefully move the pastry into the dish and press it in so that it fits snugly. Brush the inside of the pastry with some beaten egg.

Cut the cooking apples and dessert apples into slices. Place the apples in a bowl and stir in the lemon juice. Add the cinnamon, sugars, flour, vanilla extract and salt and toss together with your hands so everything is well mixed. Place the apples into the pastry case and dot the top of the fruit with the cubes of butter. Brush the outer edge of the pastry case with a little beaten egg. Roll out the remaining pastry into a circle just larger than the size of your pie dish and place over the apples. Press together the edges of the pastry base and lid with your fingers. If you want to create a pretty pattern, roll a patterned pastry tool around the edge. Trim away any excess pastry using a knife. You can re-roll this out and cut out leaf shapes to decorate the top of your pie, if you wish. Brush the top of the pie with a little more beaten egg and sprinkle with caster/granulated sugar. Cut a slit in the pie lid to let any steam out during cooking.

Bake in the preheated oven for 15 minutes, then reduce the temperature to 160°C (325°F) Gas 3 and bake for about 45 minutes more, until the pie is golden brown and the apples are soft. Remove from the oven and leave to cool for about 15 minutes, then serve immediately with custard or cream.

pie base

300 g/10½ oz. digestive biscuits/graham crackers

150 g/1¼ sticks butter, melted

caramel layer

90 g/scant ½ cup muscovado/molasses sugar

30 g/2½ tablespoons caster/granulated sugar

100 g/1 stick minus 1 tablespoon butter

400-g/14-oz. can of sweetened condensed milk

a pinch of salt

to assemble

3 bananas

freshly squeezed juice of 1 lemon

400 ml/scant 1¾ cups double/heavy cream

50 g/2 oz. plain/semisweet chocolate, grated

25-cm/10-inch springform cake pan, greased and lined

serves 8–10

Everyone loves banoffee pie – it is a quick and easy dessert to prepare and is always popular. Filled with buttery caramel and lemon-soaked bananas, and topped with chocolate curls and cream, this is delicious pie for banana lovers.

banoffee pie

Blitz the digestive biscuits/graham crackers to fine crumbs in a food processor or blender, or place in a clean plastic bag and bash with a rolling pin. Add the melted butter and stir well until all the crumbs are coated. Press the crumbs into the sides and base of the prepared pan, so that the crumbs come about 4 cm/1½ inches up the sides and will hold the filling. Press a pattern of indents into the edge using your thumb, if you like.

For the caramel layer, heat the muscovado/molasses and caster/granulated sugars in a saucepan with the butter, until the sugars and butter have melted. Add the condensed milk and salt, and cook over a gentle heat for about 10 minutes until you have a thick caramel, stirring all the time to ensure the caramel does not burn. Pour into the pie crust and leave to cool.

When you are ready to serve, peel the bananas and cut into slices and coat with the lemon juice to prevent them from browning. Place the bananas on top of the caramel. Whip the cream to soft peaks. Spoon the cream over the bananas and caramel, making sure that all the bananas are covered. Sprinkle the grated chocolate over the top of the pie before serving.

sponge

225 g/7½ oz. dates,
pitted and chopped

200 ml/scant 1 cup
boiling water

100 ml/scant ½ cup rice milk

90 g/6 tablespoons dairy-free
butter, e.g. sunflower spread

150 g/¾ cup coconut
palm sugar

3 eggs

2 tablespoons date syrup

180 g/1½ cups gluten-free
flour blend or rice flour

1 teaspoon baking powder

1 teaspoon bicarbonate of/
baking soda

1 teaspoon pure vanilla extract

pinch of sea salt

toffee sauce

100 g/3½ oz. dairy-free butter,
e.g. sunflower spread

175 g/¾ cup coconut
palm sugar

1 tablespoon
blackstrap molasses

100 ml/6 tablespoons
maple syrup

½ teaspoon pure vanilla extract

230 ml/1 cup soy cream/
creamer, plus extra to serve

pinch of sea salt

*6–8 dariole moulds,
depending on the size*

makes 6–8

A slightly lighter take on this traditional British dessert. Here, that deep, sticky toffee taste is achieved without the use of dairy, and these puddings are still wickedly good.

dairy-free sticky toffee puddings

Preheat the oven to 180°C (350°F) Gas 4.

Grease and flour the dariole moulds, then line the bases with a disc of oiled baking parchment. Set aside.

Soak the dates in the boiling water for 5 minutes, then blitz in a food processor until smooth. Add the remaining sponge ingredients and blitz again until well combined. Spoon into the prepared moulds but not right to the top, as they rise quite a bit.

Bake in the preheated oven for 20 minutes or until the sponges are risen and firm. You can check the middle with a skewer.

Meanwhile, make the toffee sauce. Melt the butter, sugar, molasses and maple syrup in a saucepan over a low heat, then simmer for a few minutes. Gradually stir in the vanilla extract, soy cream/creamer and salt and bring to the boil for 1–2 minutes until slightly thickened.

Leave the puddings in their moulds for about 5 minutes, then turn onto plates and spoon the toffee sauce over and around with a little extra soy cream/creamer to top it off.

100 g/7 tablespoons butter

150 g/5½ oz. dark/bittersweet chocolate

100 g/½ cup caster/granulated sugar

100 g/½ cup soft dark brown sugar

2 eggs

1 teaspoon pure vanilla extract

80 g/scant ⅔ cup plain/ all-purpose flour, sifted

50 g/½ cup chopped pecans

topping

150 g/⅔ cup full-fat cream cheese

160 ml/⅔ cup sour cream

50 g/¼ cup caster/ granulated sugar

1 teaspoon vanilla bean paste

2 eggs

30 g/scant ¼ cup plain/ all-purpose flour, sifted

125 g/4½ oz. dark/bittersweet chocolate, chopped

23-cm/9-inch springform cake pan, greased and lined

serves 12

Brownies and cheesecake are two items that make a regular appearance on the sweet board in pubs for good reason – they are delicious. In this recipe they are combined into one tempting dessert. As with all brownie recipes, feel free to add additional ingredients – omit the nuts if you wish, and add chocolate chips and orange zest for the perfect chocolate orange treat.

brownie cheesecake

Preheat the oven to 180°C (350°F) Gas 4.

To prepare the brownies, melt the butter and chocolate in a heatproof bowl set over a small pan of simmering water, taking care that the bottom of the bowl does not touch the water. Stir until melted, then leave to cool. In a large mixing bowl, whisk together the sugars and eggs with the vanilla until doubled in size and the mixture is very light and creamy. Slowly pour in the cooled melted chocolate mixture, whisking all the time. Fold in the flour and nuts, then pour into the prepared cake pan.

For the cheesecake topping, whisk together the cream cheese, sour cream, sugar, vanilla, eggs and flour until smooth, then stir through the chopped chocolate. Place large spoonfuls of the cheesecake mixture at intervals on top of the brownie mixture. Swirl the cheesecake and brownie mixtures together with a round-bladed knife to create swirled patterns.

Bake the cheesecake in the preheated oven for 40–45 minutes until a crust has formed on the brownie and the cheesecake mixture is set. Allow to cool before serving.

150 ml/scant ⅔ cup red wine

75 g/⅓ cup plus 2 tablespoons caster/granulated sugar, mixed with ¾ teaspoon ground cinnamon

800 g/1¾ lb. red plums, stoned/pitted and halved or quartered

crumble

60 g/3 oz. hard amaretti cookies

150 g/1 cup plus 2 tablespoons plain/all-purpose flour

75 g/⅓ cup plus 2 tablespoons caster/granulated sugar

110 g/1 stick chilled butter, cubed

double/heavy cream custard or ice cream, to serve

6 individual ovenproof dishes, greased

serves 6

The perfect afters for a weekend meal, crumble is so easy to make and always goes down a storm. The red wine in this plum crumble really increases the intensity of its plum flavour. Serve with lashings of double/heavy cream, custard or ice cream.

spiced plum, red wine and amaretti crumble

Pour the wine into a medium saucepan, add the sugar and cinnamon and warm over a low heat until the sugar has dissolved.

Bring to the boil, then reduce the heat and simmer until the liquid is reduced by just over half and is thick and syrupy. (Watch it doesn't catch and burn.)

Tip in the plums, stir, put a lid on the pan and cook for about 7–8 minutes until the plums are beginning to soften. Divide the plum mixture between the six prepared ovenproof dishes and leave to cool.

Preheat the oven to 190°C (375°F) Gas 5.

To make the crumble topping, blitz the amaretti biscuits to crumbs in a food processor, then add the flour, sugar and cubed butter and pulse until the mixture is the texture of coarse crumbs. Top the dishes with the crumble mixture and bake in the preheated oven for 20–25 minutes until the topping is crisp and the plum juices bubbling through. Serve with double/heavy cream, custard or ice cream.

index

ale: ale-battered onion rings 25
    mussels with ale and garlic 75
amaretti: spiced plum, red wine
    and amaretti crumble 140
anchovies: potato, spinach and
    anchovy bake 117
apples: braised red cabbage 42
    classic apple pie 132
aubergines: lentil moussaka 92

bacon, pastry-topped fish pie
    with 84
bake, potato, spinach and anchovy
    117
banoffee pie 135
beans: mushroom and bean chilli
    95
beef: beef short ribs 41
    beef wellington 57
    classic beef burgers 45
    Cornish pasties 31
    steak and kidney pie 58
    truffled mash cottage pie 46
    truffled mushroom lasagna 53
beer: ale-battered onion rings 25
    beer-battered cauliflower 20
    posh fish finger sandwiches 76
borlotti beans: gardener's pie 96
bread: bread and butter pudding
    129
    posh fish finger sandwiches 76
brownie cheesecake 139
burgers: classic beef burgers 45
    mushroom burgers 104
butter beans: gardener's pie 96

cabbage, braised red 42
caramel: banoffee pie 135
carrots: Cornish pasties 31
cauliflower: beer-battered
cauliflower 20
    cream of cauliflower soup 12
    individual cauli lasagnes 91
cheese: baked honey and thyme
    Camembert 28
    cheesy vegetable gratin 120
    lentil moussaka 92
    loaded jacket skins 23
    mushroom, blue cheese and
walnut quiche 99
    mushroom mac 'n' cheese 88

potato cheese pie 103
    Welsh rarebit baked potatoes
        100
cheesecake, brownie 139
chicken: best-ever roast chicken
        65
    chicken and mushroom pie 61
    chicken and parsley pearl barley
risotto 62
    chicken kievs 37
    simple roast chicken gravy 122
chillies: chilli ketchup 125
    mushroom and bean chilli 95
chocolate: brownie cheesecake
        139
chowder, cod, sweetcorn and
    prawn 15
cider: mussels with cider and
    samphire 75
clams: pastry-topped fish pie
    with bacon 84
cod: cod, sweetcorn and prawn
    chowder 15
    pastry-topped fish pie with bacon
        84
    posh fish finger sandwiches 76
condensed milk: banoffee pie
    135
Cornish pasties 31
cottage pie, truffled mash 46
courgette fries, shoestring 20
cream: banoffee pie 135
cream cheese: brownie cheesecake
        139
croutons, garlic 11
crumble, spiced plum, red wine
    and amaretti 140
curry: curry fries 19
    curry ketchup 125
    mackerel kedgeree 79

dairy-free sticky toffee puddings
        136
digestive biscuits: banoffee pie
        135

eggs: lemon meringue pie 128
    mackerel kedgeree 79
    Scotch quails' eggs 24

fish: cod, sweetcorn and prawn
chowder 15
    crispy whitebait 71
    mackerel kedgeree 79
    pastry-topped fish pie with bacon
        84
    plaice goujons 27
    posh fish finger sandwiches 76

potato, spinach and anchovy
    bake 117
potted smoked mackerel 68
saffron fish pies 80
salmon and dill pithivier 83
salmon fishcakes with watercress
    sauce 72
fries: curry fries 19
    shoestring courgette fries 20
    triple-cooked fries 108

gardener's pie 96
garlic: chicken kievs 37
    garlic croutons 11
    mussels with ale and garlic 75
    rosemary garlic potatoes 109
goujons, plaice 27
grape Yorkshire puddings 119
gratin, cheesy vegetable 120
gravy: porcini gravy 122
    red wine gravy 42, 122
    simple roast chicken gravy 122

ham: split pea and ham soup 16
herby crushed potatoes 113
hotpot, Lancashire 50

kedgeree, mackerel 79
ketchup three ways 125
kidney beans: mushroom and bean
chilli 95
kidneys: steak and kidney pie 58
kievs, chicken 37

lamb: Lancashire hotpot 50
    shepherd's pie 49
    slow-cooked lamb shanks 38
Lancashire hotpot 50
lasagna: individual cauli lasagnes
    91
    truffled mushroom lasagna 53
leeks: baby leek Yorkshire
    puddings 119
    Lancashire hotpot 50
lemon meringue pie 128
lentil moussaka 92
loaded jacket skins 23

mac 'n' cheese, mushroom 88
mackerel: mackerel kedgeree 79
    potted smoked mackerel 68
meringue pie, lemon 128
moussaka, lentil 92
mushrooms: beef wellington 57
    chicken and mushroom pie 61
    gardener's pie 96
    individual cauli lasagnes 91
    mushroom and bean chilli 95

mushroom, blue cheese and walnut quiche 99
mushroom burgers 104
mushroom mac n' cheese 88
mushroom soup 11
porcini gravy 122
truffled mash cottage pie 46
truffled mushroom lasagna 53
mussels: mussels with ale and garlic 75
mussels with cider and samphire 75
mussels with wine 75
pastry-topped fish pie with bacon 84

onion rings, ale-battered 25
oysters, steamed 32

pancetta: loaded jacket skins 23
pasta: individual cauli lasagnes 91
mushroom mac n' cheese 88
truffled mushroom lasagna 53
pasties, Cornish 31
pearl barley: chicken and parsley
pearl barley risotto 62
peas: chicken and mushroom pie 61
pies: banoffee pie 135
chicken and mushroom pie 61
classic apple pie 132
gardener's pie 96
lemon meringue pie 128
pastry-topped fish pie with bacon 84
potato cheese pie 103
saffron fish pies 80
shepherd's pie 49
steak and kidney pie 58
truffled mash cottage pie 46
pithivier, salmon and dill 83
plaice goujons 27
plums: spiced plum, red wine and amaretti crumble 140
posh fish finger sandwiches 76
potatoes: buttery crushed potatoes 113
creamy mashed potatoes 110
curry fries 19
gardener's pie 96
goose fat roast potatoes 114
herby crushed potatoes 113
Lancashire hotpot 50
loaded jacket skins 23
potato cheese pie 103
potato, spinach and anchovy bake 117

rosemary garlic potatoes 109
saffron fish pies 80
salmon fishcakes with watercress sauce 72
shepherd's pie 49
triple-cooked fries 108
truffle mash 110
truffled mash cottage pie 46
Welsh rarebit baked potatoes 100
potted smoked mackerel 68
prawns: cod, sweetcorn and prawn chowder 15
saffron fish pies 80
puff pastry: beef wellington 57
pastry-topped fish pie with bacon 84
salmon and dill pithivier 83
steak and kidney pie 58

quails' eggs, Scotch 24
quiche, mushroom, blue cheese and walnut 99

raisins: bread and butter pudding 129
rice: mackerel kedgeree 79
risotto, chicken and parsley pearl barley 62

sablé pastry: individual treacle tarts 131
saffron fish pies 80
salmon: salmon and dill pithivier 83
saffron fish pies 80
salmon fishcakes with watercress sauce 72
samphire, mussels with cider and 75
sandwiches, posh fish finger 76
sauces: gravy 42, 122
ketchup 125
tartare sauce 27
toffee sauce 136
watercress sauce 72
sausages: Scotch quails' eggs 24
toad in the hole 54
venison sausages with braised red cabbage and red wine gravy 42
Scotch quails' eggs 24
shepherd's pie 49
smoked mackerel: mackerel kedgeree 79
potted smoked mackerel 68
soups: cod, sweetcorn and

prawn chowder 15
cream of cauliflower soup 12
mushroom soup 11
split pea and ham soup 16
spiced plum, red wine and amaretti crumble 140
spinach: potato, spinach and anchovy bake 117
split pea and ham soup 16
steak and kidney pie 58
sticky toffee puddings, dairy-free 136
swede: Cornish pasties 31
sweetcorn: cod, sweetcorn and prawn chowder 15

tartare sauce 27
toad in the hole 54
toffee: dairy-free sticky toffee puddings 136
tomatoes: gardener's pie 96
individual cauli lasagnes 91
lentil moussaka 92
mushroom and bean chilli 95
tomato ketchup 125
truffled mushroom lasagna 53
treacle tarts, individual 131
truffle oil: truffle mash 110
truffled mash cottage pie 46
truffled mushroom lasagna 53
turnips: Lancashire hotpot 50

vegetables: cheesy vegetable gratin 120
venison sausages with braised red cabbage and red wine gravy 42

walnuts: mushroom, blue cheese and walnut quiche 99
watercress sauce 72
Welsh rarebit baked potatoes 100
whitebait, crispy 71
wine: beef short ribs 41
best-ever roast chicken 65
mussels with wine 75
red wine gravy 42, 122
spiced plum, red wine and amaretti crumble 140

yogurt: lentil moussaka 92
Yorkshire puddings: baby leek Yorkshire puddings 119
grape Yorkshire puddings 119

recipe credits

Miranda Ballard
Buttery crushed potatoes
Chicken kiev
Classic beef burgers with tomato
    ketchup & lettuce
Cornish pasties
Creamy mashed potatoes
Shepherds' pie
Slow-cooked lamb shanks
Steak & kidney pie

Fiona Beckett
Gravy three ways
Spiced plum, red wine
    & amaretti crumble
Venison sausages

Jordan Bourke
Dairy-free sticky toffee puddings

Tori Finch
Scotch quails' eggs

Mat Follas
Crispy whitebait
Individual treacle tarts
Mackerel kedgeree
Mussels three ways
Pastry-topped fish pie with bacon
Plaice goujons with tartare sauce
Potato, spinach & anchovy bake
Potted smoked mackerel
Salmon & dill pithivier

Emmanuel Hadjiandreau
Bread & butter pudding

Tori Haschka
Steamed oysters
Chicken & pearl barley risotto

Carol Hilker
Posh fish finger sandwiches
Ale-battered Onion rings

Vicky Jones
Lentil moussaka
Split pea & ham soup

Kathy Kordalis
Beer-battered cauliflower with
    shoestring courgette fries
Cheesy vegetable gratin
Cream of cauliflower soup
Individual cauli lasagnes
Yorkshire pudding two ways

Jenny Linford
Beef Wellington
Chicken & mushroom pie
Cod, sweetcorn & prawn chowder
Gardener's pie
Goose-fat roast potatoes
Herby crushed potatoes
Lancashire hotpot
Mushroom & bean chilli
Mushroom burgers
Mushroom mac 'n' cheese

Mushroom soup
Mushroom, blue cheese
    & walnut quiche
Potato cheese pie
Rosemary garlic potatoes
Saffron fish pies
Salmon fishcakes with
    watercress sauce
Triple-cooked fries
Truffle mash
Truffled mash cottage pie
Truffled mushroom lasagne

Hannah Miles
Banoffee pie
Brownie cheesecake
Classic apple pie
Lemon meringue pie
Loaded jacket skins
Toad in the hole
Welsh rarebit jacket potatoes

Laura Santini
Best-ever roast chicken
Beef short ribs

Jenny Tschiesche
Baked honey & thyme Camembert
    with crudités

Laura Washburn
Curry fries
Ketchup three ways
Braised red cabbage

picture credits

Peter Cassidy Pages 4, 5, 8, 9, 25, 35, 67, 77, 87, 107.

Mowie Kay Pages 13, 21, 43, 90, 118, 120, 122, 126, 141.

Steve Painter Pages 18, 22, 24, 26, 29, 30, 36, 39, 48, 59, 69, 70, 74, 78, 82, 85, 101, 116, 124, 130, 133, 134, 138.

Con Poulos Pages 40, 64.

William Reavell Pages 17, 34, 55, 93.

Kate Whitaker Page 137.

Isobel Wield Pages 33, 63.

Clare Winfield Pages 10, 14, 44, 47, 51, 52, 56, 60, 66, 73, 81, 86, 89, 94, 97, 98, 103, 105, 106, 108, 109, 111, 113, 115.